About this Learning Guide

Shmoop Will Make You a Better Lover*
*of Literature, History, Poetry, Life...

Our lively learning guides are written by experts and educators who want to show your brain a good time. Shmoop writers come primarily from Ph.D. programs at top universities, including Stanford, Harvard, and UC Berkeley.

Want more Shmoop? We cover literature, poetry, bestsellers, music, US history, civics, biographies (and the list keeps growing). Drop by our website to see the latest.

www.shmoop.com

Table of Contents

Introduction

In a Nutshell

As You Like It is a comedy written by <u>William Shakespeare</u> in late 1599 or early 1600. It is a love story taking place in the forest and featuring multiple couples falling in love. The primary romance is one of convoluted deception as the play's heroine, Rosalind, dresses up like a man (called "Ganymede") and teases the play's hero, Orlando, for being in love with Rosalind – while she herself has actually fallen in love with Orlando.

As You Like It is one of Shakespeare's more popular comedies, and is known for its heavy romantic element. You may have heard the play's most famous speech, which begins with "All the world's a stage, / And all the men and women merely players." In addition to being a witty commentary on life, this famous quote is also a good summation of all the coupling that goes on in *As You Like It*. Everyone is playing everyone else, and with all the marriages at the end, you bet there's going to be some fun throughout. *As You Like It* is also rather well known from the feminist angle, as its heroine (Rosalind) is one of Shakespeare's most fleshed-out female characters.

Why Should I Care?

As You Like It is a special work of literature because it doesn't particularly care if you care or not. That's the whole point of the play – life is this or that, depending on how you look at it, and how you look at it is your prerogative.

The work is a rare chance to see people at their finest because they're honest about who they are. Rosalind delights in juxtaposition, so she dresses up like a man; Touchstone doesn't care who thinks he's foolish. Jaques just wants to be miserable, and so he is. With the possible exception of Orlando's jealous brother, this play is all about being true to yourself, no matter how anybody else judges or thinks of you.

Amidst all these lofty topics of individuality, perception, social obligations and the like, the play has one character that embodies the mingling of the life of the mind and the life of the heart. Rosalind is the perfect example of someone who functions on intuition rather than intention. She doesn't need to declare her beliefs or perspective – she just *is* them.

Yale professor and literary critic <u>Harold Bloom</u> credits Rosalind with being the first real lover in all of modern literature. She's the first to make fun of love, and also the first to let herself be fully embraced by all its frivolity and pure joy. Bloom says "Rosalind is unique […] in Western drama, because it is so difficult to achieve a perspective upon her that she herself does not anticipate and share." Basically, this girl is incredibly self-aware. As a woman, Rosalind's character doesn't *need* to have all the drama and oomph of Shakespeare's male protagonists, yet she's memorable because she's so *unexpected*.

It's not for nothing that Rosalind has the most lines of any of Shakespeare's female

characters; outside of the trappings of what *women* are supposed to be, she can enact the best of being a *person*, full of foibles but also capable of incredible insight. The best way to get at Rosalind is to realize she's one of Shakespeare's only characters that you'd actually like to be with while trapped in an elevator. Hamlet might bore you to death, and Macbeth might cut out your liver and send it to your mother, but Rosalind would probably play a game of travel Scrabble with you and then ask for your number with a wink.

Rosalind's attitude and the breadth of her perspective color the whole play, which doesn't come to any big decisions about what type of life is best. Court or country, fool or scholar, duke or exile – these are all just different ways to live, none better than the other. By having all of these different characters live the vastly unique lives they want to lead, Shakespeare reminds us that no two people choose the same two paths – and that's OK. Yes, we've all heard "different strokes for different folks," but while you were busy embracing all the colors of the rainbow, Shakespearean literature was making the point in a far more eloquent manner and with 90% less eye-rolling.

So *As You Like It* is a healthy reminder of what is best put in the words of yet another great poet: Dr. Seuss. You should "be who you are and say what you feel, because those who mind don't matter and those who matter don't mind." So wear your multi-colored toe-socks and dye your hair pink if it makes you happy.

Summary

Book Summary

Orlando's dad, Sir Rowland de Boys has died, leaving behind three sons: Oliver, Jaques, and Orlando. Orlando's a good kid, well-liked and virtuous, which of course irks his big brother. Although Oliver is supposed to take care of Orlando, he treats his little bro poorly, which in turn irks his little bro. Orlando wants to run away, but he's not sure where he would go.

Meanwhile, this girl named Rosalind is living with her cousin Celia and Celia's dad, Duke Frederick. Like Orlando, Rosalind has lost her father, Duke Senior; her uncle, Duke Frederick, has banished him. Duke Senior formerly ruled the land, but now that he's banished, his new home is the Forest of Arden. Rosalind, surprisingly, was allowed to stay at court with her cousin Celia. The two cousins love each other dearly, and Duke Frederick knew that if he banished Rosalind along with Duke Senior, Celia would follow her into exile. Because he didn't want to lose his daughter, the Duke let Rosalind stay.

Rosalind and Orlando first meet at a wrestling match where Orlando has come to challenge the formidable court wrestler, Charles – maybe to die, because Orlando feels so miserable and worthless. Against all expectations, Orlando wins the wrestling match, and he and Rosalind fall in love as quickly as it takes you to make Ramen noodles. Though they don't exchange a lot of words, Rosalind gives Orlando her necklace as a token of love or whatever.

But just as the wrestling match sparks their enchantment, it also provokes their banishment.

Oliver is angry that Orlando will be even *more* popular since winning the match, so he plans to murder his brother once he gets home. (Sibling rivalry on a whole new level, isn't it?) Adam, the old family servant, learns of Oliver's plot and warns Orlando before he reaches home. To escape Oliver's treachery, Orlando decides to take Adam and Adam's life savings with him and head for the woods.

While the rich are taking from the poor, Rosalind finds Duke Frederick in a bad mood; he was happy for the young champion until he learned that Orlando is the son of Sir Rowland de Boys, one of his former enemies. Duke Frederick, stormy and upset, takes out his frustrations on Rosalind. He accuses her of being a traitor and threatens to have her killed if she stays at court. On that cue, Rosalind decides to leave for the forest, and Celia of course pledges to go with her. To avoid being the target of thieves, Rosalind decides she'll dress as a boy named Ganymede, and Celia will become Ganymede's "sister" Aliena. They agree to take Touchstone, the court fool, with them, too, possibly for entertainment along the way.

Cut to the Forest of Arden, where we meet Rosalind's dad, Duke Senior. He's a pretty happy-go-lucky guy for being a banished duke, and he reflects on the wonder of living in nature while everyone else suffers under the rules of being "royal" at court. Orlando, making good progress in the starving department, along with his faithful servant Adam, runs into a banquet being hosted by the Duke in the forest, and threatens to kill everyone if they do not give him something to eat, like, now. The Duke is all "chill out, and bring Adam, too" so all those merry ex-courtiers become Orlando's friends. We also meet Duke Senior's courtier, Jaques, who is the downer of the century what with his philosophizing and constant melancholy.

On the cross-dressing front, things are good for Rosalind/Ganymede as she too settles into the Forest of Arden. She has met a shepherd, Corin, who leads Ganymede to buy his master's house. Soon, Ganymede (Rosalind), Aliena (Celia), and Touchstone have gotten all familiar with a bunch of country characters. Among them are Silvius, a poor, love-stricken shepherd, and Phebe, the woman he loves that unfortunately hates him in return.

Yet love is definitely in the air. Rosalind discovers poems (stuck to trees) that a mysterious lover has penned – about her (Rosalind, not the fake man). They're pretty awful in the literary accomplishment sense, but when Celia comes to the natural conclusion that Orlando is in the forest and therefore the author, Rosalind goes into a fit of excitement. Rosalind hatches a completely nonsensical plan to harass and subsequently (somehow) reel in the poor, lovesick Orlando.

Rosalind soon meets Orlando in the forest, still in her disguise as Ganymede. After some talk about the poems and the tragedy of the author's situation, Orlando confesses that he is indeed the writer. Rosalind (as Ganymede) pretends she's got a lot of experience breaking people of their lovesickness, and promises Orlando if he'll visit "him" as Ganymede, Ganymede will pretend to be Rosalind. As such, "she" will abuse Orlando in the way only girlfriends can, until he wants nothing more to do with Rosalind, or really women at all. Orlando agrees, thinking he'll instead prove that his love for Rosalind can't be beat. So begins a convoluted courtship where a girl pretending to be a boy pretends to be a girl with the actual boy who loves her – so she can simultaneously flirt with and torture him while she deepens her love.

Celia harasses Rosalind for being pathetically in love, and Rosalind as Ganymede harasses Orlando for the same. Ganymede also harasses the shepherd girl Phebe (with whom Silvius is in love), who meanwhile has actually fallen in love with Ganymede because he's so sharp with her. As all of this is happening, Touchstone has managed to get around the forest and find a nice shepherd girl, Audrey, who is not too bright or beautiful, but willing enough to get married to him.

The action all comes to a head when Oliver, Orlando's brother, shows up and meets Ganymede and Celia with a bloody hanky he's been sent to give Ganymede as a token from Orlando. Oliver originally had been sent to the forest by Duke Frederick, who wanted Oliver to find Orlando and kill him. Oliver had mean intentions, but unexpected events threw a wrench in the plan: Orlando found his brother first. While Oliver napped under a tree, a snake found him and prepared to bite. Orlando scared away the snake, and then stuck around to fight a lioness that was lying in wait to eat Oliver.

Orlando's selfless actions so affect Oliver that he has a total change of heart; he now loves his brother and no longer wants to kill him. This is good news, because Oliver and Celia fall in love (about two minutes after meeting, in true Shakespearean ridiculousness). Ganymede and the wounded Orlando confer over how odd it will be to have their "siblings" marry after such a short meeting, and Orlando confides in Ganymede that he'll miss Rosalind even more as he watches his brother gain the happiness he can't have. Rosalind (as Ganymede) then promises that Orlando will marry his ladylove the next day. Ganymede makes the same promise to deliver happiness to Phebe (who wants to marry Ganymede) and to Silvius (who's sick with love over Phebe). Ganymede does all this with the following clever device: she gets them all to agree that if Rosalind appears, Orlando will marry her, if Ganymede ever marries a woman, he will marry Phebe, but if Phebe doesn't marry Ganymede, she must marry Silvius. This way everyone will be happy – except for Phebe, who's getting tricked into a marriage to Silvius.

The wedding day comes, and everyone is waiting around to see how Ganymede can possibly pull this off. Then Hymen, the god of marriage, conveniently appears with a now completely feminine Rosalind. Rosalind says "hi" to her father, promises to give herself to Orlando, and everyone falls into dancing and feasting over the four marriages: Phebe to Silvius, Audrey to Touchstone, Celia to Oliver, and Rosalind to Orlando.

Jaques de Boys, Orlando and Oliver's *other* brother, shows up during the dancing with good news. Duke Frederick had planned to invade the forest and kill everyone, but thankfully he met a nice old religious guy at the edge of the forest who convinced him to change his mind and instead give up his court position and worldly possessions. (Ha!) Jaques, Duke Senior's courtier (who happens to have the same name as the de Boys brother), will join Duke Frederick in his hermit-like studies. For now, though, everyone else is free to party like they're in a forest. Soon enough, they will all return to the court, where Duke Senior can get his title back and everyone else can live happily ever after without banishment and with thorough revelry, as everybody likes it.

Act I, Scene i

- Orlando, son of Sir Rowland de Boys, is in a bad way. We meet him in the midst of his complaints to Adam, an old family servant. Orlando's father has died, and his older brother, Oliver, is neglectful and hurtful. Oliver is in charge of giving Orlando good "breeding," but Oliver makes Orlando eat with the laborers and doesn't give him the education that courtly gentleman should have.
- Orlando resolves to do something about this, which turns out to be trying to wring Oliver's neck while making demands. Orlando wants to be educated and treated like a gentleman (as their father wished), or else Oliver should hand over Orlando's inheritance and let him do what he pleases.
- Orlando lets Oliver go, but we're not sure what will come next.
- After Adam and Orlando leave, Oliver is joined by Charles, the court wrestler, and also a regular court gossip. We learn that the old Duke Senior has been banished by his younger brother, the new Duke Frederick. Banished Duke Senior has been followed by a bunch of young gentlemen, and all have been making merry together in the Forest of Arden, Robin Hood-style.
- Charles tells us that Duke Senior's daughter, Rosalind, was not banished, but is instead staying with her cousin Celia (Duke Frederick's daughter) because the two are practically in love (in a cousinly manner).
- Charles gets to the point of his visit: tomorrow there's a big wrestling match, and Oliver's little brother Orlando is jonesing to fight Charles. Charles worries that Orlando is "young and tender," so he's come to get Oliver to forbid his younger brother from fighting.
- Oliver sees his chance – he tells Charles he's already tried to persuade Orlando away from wrestling (a lie), and that Orlando is a villain and traitor (also a lie – someone's pants are soon to be on fire). Charles is convinced, and Oliver has an aside in which we learn he hates Orlando because Orlando doesn't really have faults – he's a pretty good guy.
- Oliver leaves to make sure Orlando fights and is crushed in tomorrow's match.

Act I, Scene ii

- We meet Celia and Rosalind. Rosalind is a little miffed that her father, Duke Senior, has been banished by Duke Frederick (her uncle and Celia's dad).
- Celia recommends that Rosalind change her perspective and think of Duke Frederick as her new dad. This doesn't fly, as Rosalind doesn't need two dads and is hanging onto a nifty thing called family loyalty.
- The girls decide to distract themselves with frippery, so they talk about love and fortune. Celia notes it's a pity that only ugly girls are honest, which Rosalind believes to be more about nature than fortune.
- The cousins go back and forth on nature and fortune before being interrupted by Touchstone, the court fool. He's come to bring Celia to her father, but instead gets caught up in a talk about the ease swearing on your honor when you have no honor.
- Le Beau, a courtier of Duke Frederick, comes in to tell the women that Charles (remember the court wrestler?) has just fought three strong brothers and in general leaves broken ribs

scattered in his wake. The next wrestling match, Charles vs. Orlando, is about to go down right where the women are standing, in case they'd like to stay and watch the carnage.

- Then Duke Frederick (Celia's father, Rosalind's uncle) enters and tries to get the girls to convince young Orlando not to fight, as he's terribly outmatched by the beast of a man who broke all the ribs.
- The girls plead with Orlando, but he replies he just wants their good wishes, as it doesn't matter if he dies. No one would mourn him anyway, he says, including himself. The girls ignore what he's saying, but they are moved by his good looks and fortitude.
- Because he's a main character and there are several more scenes left to go, Orlando easily beats Charles, who can't even speak when cocky Orlando wants to fight again. Duke Frederick is impressed with Orlando, until he finds out the boy is son of his enemy, Sir Rowland de Boys. Rosalind is glad for the news, as Sir Rowland was a good friend of her banished father, Duke Senior (also an enemy of Duke Frederick).
- Celia and Rosalind congratulate Orlando and Rosalind, nursing a crush, gives Orlando her necklace as a token. They clearly make eyes at each other, and Orlando, indeed "young and tender," can't even manage to talk to Rosalind.
- The googly eyes are broken up by Le Beau, who warns Orlando that the Duke is in a bad mood and might harm Orlando if he sticks around. Orlando asks about the ladies he's just met, and learns that Rosalind is Duke Senior's daughter.
- Meanwhile, Duke Frederick, who has been keeping Rosalind at his house, begins to weary of the fact that everyone keeps praising her. He decides that what's good for the father is good for the daughter; he'll soon banish Rosalind, too.
- Orlando heads home to his scheming brother, and is still in the early blush of loving Rosalind.

Act I, Scene iii

- Rosalind and Celia engage in some girl talk, where Rosalind is clearly in an emotional state over Orlando.
- Celia marvels that Rosalind could fall in love so quickly, and Rosalind points out that Orlando's dad and her dad were good friends, so (obviously) her love makes complete sense.
- This chatter is interrupted by Celia's father, Duke Frederick, who's still storming and dishing out threats of death and destruction. Duke Frederick tells Rosalind that if she doesn't leave the court immediately, he'll have her killed.
- But before she hits the old dusty trail of banishment, Rosalind wants to know why she's being sent off.
- Duke Frederick lamely claims that Rosalind must leave because she's likely to become a traitor, just like her father. (This is curious, as her father wasn't actually a traitor.)
- As Celia pleads for Rosalind, it becomes clear that the Duke is actually jealous of how people look at Rosalind. Duke Frederick tells Celia that she'll look more attractive once her cousin is gone. He emphasizes Rosalind's death sentence once more before going on his merry way.
- Understandably, the girls are bummed. This lasts for two minutes before they hatch a plan

to run away together to the Forest of Arden where Duke Senior (Celia's uncle/Rosalind's dad) lives with his merry band.
- Rosalind points out that girls traveling alone are a sure invitation to robbing and rape. Celia says maybe they should make themselves look dirty, so they won't attract male attention.
- Rosalind has a better idea. She concludes that because she is the taller of the two, she should dress as a man. Rosalind decides to be called Ganymede, after the young boy who was Jove's cupbearer. Celia decides on the name Aliena, which means "the estranged one" in Latin (think "alien") and is a clever reference to Celia's state of self-banishment.
- The girls decide to take along Touchstone, the court fool.
- Celia declares that they go not to banishment, but to liberty. (By Jove, a motif!)

Act II Scene i

- Back at the forest Duke Senior, his attending Lord Amiens, and various forest-folks are getting ready to hunt for some dinner.
- Duke Senior strikes us as a jovial kind of guy – he waxes on about how the forest suits him because it doesn't flatter and lie like the court. The winter bites him as it does anybody else, so he knows here that everyone is truly equal. In the forest, with its egalitarian treatment of all people, the Duke is safe and can trust that the world is all good.
- As Duke Senior gets ready to hunt some venison, he comments that it irks him a little to kill the native residents of the forest (the animals). One of the lords raises the point that Jaques, yet another of Senior's attending lords, was recently talking about just that. And now we get to hear all about it via the lord's re-telling.
- Here we go. Jaques spotted a deer that had been injured but not killed by a hunter. He then spent a good amount of time lamenting in this vein: the forest belongs to the animals, which were there first. To kill them is to be no better than the usurping Duke Frederick that stole Duke Senior's kingdom. Jaques made all these long comments while standing by and watching the deer suffer and cry. He resented other deer passers-by for trotting on past their fallen comrade. Jaques compared the deer's deliberate ignorance of their fellow deer's suffering to the mean manner of the court.
- That's it for the tale. The Duke, hearing of Jaques's suffering, says he'd like to go and see the guy, because it's fun to converse with him when he's in this profound melancholy state (which, it turns out, is always).

Act II, Scene ii

- Duke Frederick is having a conniption because no one is confessing about seeing Rosalind and Celia run away together. Frederick concludes that some court members were in on the girls' escape, and is informed that Touchstone the fool is also missing.
- One of Celia's maids speculates that Orlando probably went off with the girls as well, considering he so pleased them with his brawny display.
- Duke Frederick demands that Orlando be brought to him, and if Orlando is nowhere to be

found, then his brother Oliver should be brought in find the young man.

Act II, Scene iii

- Orlando is on his way back to Oliver's house when he meets Adam, their family servant.
- Adam says Oliver has heard about Orlando's victory and is concerned about the effect it's going to have on the ever-growing Orlando Fan Club. Oliver plans to burn down Orlando's lodging, which wouldn't be so bad if he didn't plan on Orlando being in it at the time.
- Orlando doesn't know where to go. Even if he ran away, he'd have to do something drastic, like become a highway robber, to support himself, which isn't appealing to him.
- Adam, kind and elderly, has some money he's been stashing away for retirement (500 crowns) and he offers his life savings to Orlando, suggesting that they could live on it awhile if they ran away together.
- Orlando notes Adam is an old-school servant, serving for duty and not money, which is a compliment. Orlando decides the two will leave together and settle for a simple life.
- Adam says he's lived at Sir Rowland's from age seventeen to now, when he's almost 80, and he'll be glad to leave and die well, without being indebted to any master.

Act II, Scene iv

- Rosalind, dressed as Ganymede, Celia, as Aliena, and Touchstone have all arrived in the Forest of Arden. They jest with each other about their tired state as two real forest people wander into the scene, deep in conversation.
- Corin, an old man, is counseling a young man, Silvius, on love. Silvius is madly infatuated with a woman named Phebe, and like many people madly in love, Silvius has 1) no sense and 2) no likely chance. He wanders off indulging in his own absurdity, and Rosalind sighs that she shares the same wound as Silvius.
- Touchstone also shares the wound of madness (yes, the love-induced kind), and goes on about a woman he loves. He puns and plays with love, and Celia breaks up the chatter by pointing out that, while all of this is very nice, she is kind of on the verge of starving to death.
- The three end up talking with Corin (the old man), who says he doesn't have anything to give, as his master is a miser and also selling the property where Corin tends his flock. Silvius is supposed to buy the property, but is too distracted by to make the purchase. Given this, Rosalind (as Ganymede) says she'll buy cottage, pasture, flock, and all. Celia, ever-thoughtful, says they will increase Corin's pay, and they'll all live happily together.

Act II, Scene v

- Amiens (another lord attending Duke Senior) enters singing a song about happy nature and contented people.
- Jaques begs him to keep singing, though Amiens counters it will only make Jaques more melancholy. Since Jaques is happy to be melancholy, he insists Amiens sing on.
- Amiens points out the Duke has been looking for Jaques all day, and Jaques points out he's been avoiding the Duke all day.
- Jaques sings a mean little verse he's made up about men's foolishness for leaving the court, and announces he'll sleep while Amiens finds the Duke to come to the evening's banquet.

Act II, Scene vi

- Adam, the old servant of the de Boys, is in the forest with the young Orlando. Adam, now feeling as though he's dying from hunger, bids farewell to his master, as he must prepare his grave.
- Orlando gives a hearty talk to Adam, and promises if anything lives in this "desert," then Orlando will bring it for Adam to eat.
- He asks that Adam hold off on dying until he gets back, as dying earlier would be an insult to Orlando's hard labor.

Act II, Scene vii

- Duke Senior and the merry men are readying to settle down to dinner.
- Jaques arrives shortly, full of good humor. (Amazing!) Jaques ran into a fool in the forest, who reflected on the passing of time as a merciless march. But the fool's musings were so simple and un-profound that Jaques thought the whole situation was hilarious.
- Jaques says the man was a courtier (sounds like Touchstone to us).
- Jaques feels overwhelmed by the sheer volume of observations crammed in the fool's mind – though the fool speaks of his observations in "mangled" or confusing ways.
- Jaques wishes to be such a fool. He clarifies that his only virtue is his wisdom. Jaques points out that only funny men have the real power to point out the foolishness of the wise (or supposedly wise), and that the double-edged sword is such that, should a wise man ignore a fool's brilliant point, he'll only seem more stupid.
- Duke Senior isn't buying it, content and happy as he is, and he essentially calls Jaques a hypocrite for pretending to be such a serious and wise man. He calls out the fact that Jaques, in his day, used to have a little fun on the town, too.
- Jaques points out that sinning is universal; therefore, he doesn't attack any particular individual at any particular time, but generally rails on about humans in general. He just hates everyone equally.
- Thankfully, Orlando breaks up all the deep and hateful thoughts by charging in with his

- sword drawn, demanding that no one eat anything.
- Jaques calls him a cock (no kidding) and Duke Senior asks whether Orlando is distressed or just raised to have no manners.
- Orlando is hell-bent on stabbing somebody if they eat, though the Duke insists he should take it easy.
- Orlando *can't* take it easy, because he and Adam are starving. But he does apologize, saying everything in the forest is so brutish, he must have become brutish himself.
- The Duke understands, and he invites Orlando to eat with them. Everyone promises to wait while Orlando runs off to get Adam.
- Duke Senior takes the opportunity to comment on how nice it is that everybody is unhappy, not just them.
- Jaques then makes the speech beginning "All the world's a stage, and all the men and women merely players." He goes on to detail the seven ages of man, as follows: You start as an infant, then a whining schoolboy, progress to a lover, then a soldier, then a "justice" or contented middle-aged man, followed by the kind-of-old guy with spectacles, and finally the very, very old guy who has lost his senses and is dead to the world.
- Jaques's speech is interrupted when Orlando enters with Adam.
- The Duke won't bother them with questions before eating, so they eat heartily as Amiens sings another song about birds and flowers and his other favorite things.
- During the song, Orlando whispers to Duke Senior that he is the son of Sir Rowland de Boys. The Duke recognizes Rowland's features in the boy and is delighted to have him. Duke Senior was a good friend of Sir Rowland, so he welcomes Orlando and Adam to his cave even more heartily.
- The Duke wishes to hear the story of how Adam and Orlando ended up homeless and hungry in the forest.

Act III, Scene i

- Back at the Court, Frederick is still in a rage trying to find Orlando. He's seized Oliver and demands that he find Orlando and bring him back within a year, alive or dead. As usual, should Oliver fail, the punishment is banishment.
- In the meantime, Duke Frederick's tough guys have seized all of Oliver's land and things.
- Oliver replies to the Duke by proclaiming he's never loved his brother Orlando (thinking that, if the Duke and he have a common enemy, they might get on a little better). The Duke, less than interested in being pals, says hating his brother makes Oliver even more of a villain. (Slightly ironic considering what he did to Duke Senior, isn't it?)
- Duke Frederick sends Oliver packing.

Act III, Scene ii

- Orlando busies himself with hanging poems on the trees of the forest, all dedicated to his love for Rosalind.

- Corin and Touchstone enter, bantering as usual. Corin asks how Touchstone likes living in the forest, and Touchstone doesn't give him a straight answer. Corin, by contrast, talks earnestly about nature's simplicity and all of his favorite things.
- After Corin's beautiful speech, Touchstone asks Corin if he's ever been to court. Hearing that Corin hasn't, Touchstone decrees that Corin is damned.
- The fool goes on to suggest that not visiting court means never having learned good manners, no good manners mean wickedness, wickedness is sin, and sin leads to damnation.
- Touchstone is about to light into Corin for making a living "by the copulation of cattle." Thankfully, Rosalind interrupts as she enters, dressed as Ganymede and reading a paper.
- Rosalind reads out some particularly bad poetry praising Rosalind's virtues and good looks, which Touchstone counters with his own bad verse. Mimicking the poems on the paper, Touchstone compares Rosalind to the kind of girl you *don't* bring home to Mom.
- As Touchstone teases, Celia enters, reading the same terrible love poems found on the tree.
- Rosalind agrees that the poetry is awful, and Celia, clearly seeing some girl-talk is in order, sends Touchstone off with Corin so the two girls can titter.
- After the tittering, it becomes clear to Celia that Rosalind hasn't figured out one important fact: the poems have obviously been written by Orlando.
- Celia teases as Rosalind pleads and begs to know who it is that's fawning over her so foolishly (and inarticulately). On discovering that Orlando is responsible, Rosalind is excitedly foolish. Mostly, she is desperate to find out what Orlando's been up to, and most importantly, whether he knows she's been dithering about the forest dressed as a boy.
- Just as Celia and Rosalind are fussing with each other over love, guess who should come traipsing through the forest? It's not just a plot device; it's a hero!
- Orlando and Jaques are traipsing and bickering together. There's some chiding on both sides – Jaques thinks Orlando a fool of love, and Orlando suggests Jaques should…drown himself. They take leave of each other, and Jaques exits.
- Seeing her chance, Rosalind, dressed as a man, plots with Celia to speak to Orlando as a "saucy lackey."
- Rosalind, indeed going for the saucy lackey bit, ambles up and asks Orlando what o'clock it is, in a sassy fashion. He replies, like a genius, that there's no clock in the forest, which lets Ganymede launch into a dissertation about how a lover who loved true could tell time easily – by his heart sighing every minute and groaning every hour.
- Then she proposes that time moves differently for different people, complete with examples that are especially interesting for their language and thus boring to summarize. You should think about reading them.
- Orlando asks the "boy" where he lives and Ganymede claims to live with his "sister," meaning Celia (disguised as Aliena). Ganymede claims that though he was raised in the forest, he picked up his courtly accent from his uncle, a court-raised man who fled from the court and women in love. Ganymede claims his uncle thought women were particularly infected by foolishness and had so many evils that none outweighed the other.
- Ganymede complains of the idiot that is leaving bad poems to some girl "Rosalind" on all of the trees. He claims that if he met the young fool so caught up in love, he'd advise him out of it.
- Orlando, taking the bait, admits he's the love-struck poet and asks for Ganymede's remedy.

- Ganymede quips that Orlando can't possibly be a prisoner of love, as he wears none of the marks Ganymede's courtly uncle described as "embossed sores." Orlando lacks a lean cheek, sunken eye, neglected beard, and all manner of disheveled clothing. Ganymede points out Orlando is so well preened that he's clearly enamored of himself as much as anyone else – not exactly the mark of a lovesick idiot. (So, now Ganymede is complimenting Orlando's appearance, which is probably as close to hitting on him as Rosalind's going to get.)
- Orlando simply replies he can convince Ganymede of his love for Rosalind, and Ganymede assures he can cure him of love.
- The plan unfurls. Ganymede claims he's cured another man of love by having the man visit him every day, to pretend the "boy" was his mistress. Ganymede (pretending to be the girl) abused him with all the attitude you'd only tolerate when in love. Eventually, Ganymede gave him so much grief that the poor guy gave up to live as a monk.
- Orlando claims that such a tactic wouldn't cure him of his love for Rosalind, which obviously means he'll show up at Ganymede's house every day and woo him (her) to prove it.
- Ganymede, pleased at this outcome, agrees. He says Orlando must call him Rosalind from now on, which is so very fitting and so very, very weird at the same time.
- The plan is a success: Rosalind can keep up her disguise and still get the affections of her crush, Orlando. Orlando gets sexy with a guy, but only to escape the love of a woman. So Orlando becomes embroiled in a farce of a love affair – which, in reality, is not a farce at all.

Act III, Scene iii

- Touchstone has been busy finding love of his own with Audrey, a simple shepherd girl. He intends to marry her.
- As Touchstone fawns over Audrey, Jaques follows. Touchstone woos Audrey with pretty words about poetry and honesty. That's all good, except when we said Audrey was simple, we meant *simple*. To put it, well, simply, Audrey doesn't get his poetry, it's over her head. But Touchstone is fine with that.
- To give you a touch of their bandying, Audrey says she is grateful to the gods that she is foul (ugly), because it means she isn't promiscuous. Touchstone replies he's glad too, and perhaps if they're lucky, "sluttishness may come hereafter." (That's a quote. Seriously.)
- Touchstone announces that a local vicar, Sir Oliver Martext, has promised to meet the pair in the forest and marry them. So they're making this happen. Like, right now.
- Touchstone then has a long speech about horns. (In Shakespeare's day, there was an awful lot of punning about horns, referring to men who are "cuckolded.")
- We'd like to take this opportunity to bring you a HISTORICAL CONTEXT LESSON: We know it's a funny term, but "cuckolded" comes from the Old French for "cuckoo," as the cuckoo was notorious for laying her eggs in other birds' nests without their knowledge, like a woman might have a man take care of her during pregnancy, without revealing that the child wasn't his. Other birds wouldn't figure out that the eggs weren't theirs until they'd

already hatched the cuckoo babies. The term originally referred to a man whose wife was sleeping around without his knowledge, but can be generally applied to any man being taken advantage of or controlled by a woman. You'll get a kick out of some more word history here.

- Anyway, Touchstone is interrupted from the cuckold-containing speech when Sir Oliver Martext, the vicar, shows up. The vicar refuses to marry the couple if no one is there to give away the bride.
- Jaques, who has not left yet, agrees to stand up and give Audrey away. Glad we got that little formality nailed down.
- And yet, we're still not good to go. Jaques points out that Touchstone is a man of the court, and it isn't really fitting that he be married under a bush.
- Touchstone gives us a saucy aside; if he isn't properly married, it will be easier to leave his wife. Touchstone calls Audrey away, they'll have to wait a little longer to get married.

Act III, Scene iv

- Still in the forest with Celia, Rosalind swoons for a bit over Orlando, who has such pretty red-brown hair. Celia notes that his hair is the same color as that of Judas (the disciple who betrayed Jesus in the Bible).
- Rosalind is upset – Orlando promised to show up that morning to woo "Ganymede" and still hasn't arrived. Celia suggests that maybe he's loyal when he's in love, but he's not in love right now, even with Rosalind.
- Celia points out that love is fickle, and tells Rosalind she heard that Orlando has been passing time in the forest with the exiled Duke Senior, Rosalind's own father.
- Rosalind, you may have noticed, has not mentioned seeing her dad yet, and now she tells us she met him yesterday, joked with him a little bit, and left, never revealing she was actually his daughter and not a country boy.
- She sighs that there's no reason to discuss her father when there's Orlando to discuss instead.
- As Rosalind moons about being love-struck, Corin enters and asks them if they'd like to see a funny scene: a faithful lover being scorned and destroyed. They'll get this tasty little entertainment treat if they just follow him. Rosalind is eager to see it, as at the moment she's all about love and scheming her own involvement in others' affairs.

Act III, Scene v

- Rosalind and Celia look on at Silvius and Phebe.
- Silvius is pretty pathetic. He says Phebe may not love him, but he asks her to at least not be so bitter about the whole thing. Phebe replies that Silvius claimed her eyes could kill. He has lied, because she has tried to kill him with her eyes and he's still around. (Ouch.)
- Silvius says the wounds made by Cupid's arrows are invisible, and Phebe just tells him, in essence, "Go away."

- Rosalind enters the discussion as Ganymede, still the saucy lackey. "He" tells Phebe she really shouldn't be so insulting to poor Silvius, as 1) she's not that cute, and 2) she should be grateful that anybody likes her, as she has "bugle eyeballs."
- Ganymede chides Silvius, as he is worth more as a man than Phebe's worth as a woman.
- Ganymede then gives some advice to Phebe: "Sell when you can, you are not for all markets." Now *that's* showing your claws.
- Phebe begins to swoon over Ganymede, attracted by the fact that he's a jerk who is totally disinterested in (if not hateful of) her existence. Phebe says she'd rather hear Ganymede scorn than Silvius woo.
- Ganymede runs off, insisting that Phebe should be kind and take Silvius, and thinking "Oh no."
- Phebe, maybe to appease Ganymede, claims to love Silvius in a neighborly manner, but not as a lover.
- Phebe hatches a plan to get Silvius to help her win over Ganymede. Because Silvius is desperately in love, he'll do whatever she wants. Phebe's interest has been sparked by Ganymede's scorn, and while she claims to "love him not" she also "hates him not," which leaves a lot of room for wiggles.
- Phebe decides to write a letter to Ganymede, which she'll have Silvius deliver.

Act IV, Scene i

- Rosalind, as Ganymede, chats with Jaques about his melancholy. Jaques thinks that a solid approach to life is to be sad and silent, and Ganymede claims he might as well be a fencepost.
- Jaques then details different types of melancholy, and Rosalind identifies his as the melancholy of travelers.
- Rosalind looks into this particular melancholy of travelers. She understands why Jaques would be sad: in traveling, he gets to see what everyone else has; yet to travel, he's had to give up everything of his own.
- The philosophizing gets cut short when Orlando shows up – about an hour late.
- Rosalind, as Ganymede, is rather temperamental (putting on an impression of a woman) – first upset at Orlando for being late, then in the mood to be loved and chatted up.
- Orlando says he would start the conversation with a kiss, if Ganymede were his lover. Ganymede contends that kisses in conversations are saved for those moments when lovers have run out of stuff to talk about, and, if kisses be denied, then that's something to talk about too.
- There's more cajoling, and Orlando threatens to die from love if "Rosalind" will not have him. Ganymede playing Rosalind (who is Rosalind playing Ganymede) points out that men die from a lot of things, but rarely from love.
- This bantering ends with Ganymede suggesting that Aliena (Celia) play priest and marry the couple, the couple being Rosalind playing Ganymede playing Rosalind, and Orlando.
- They fake vows, and Rosalind points out that it's great to be in love with women, but when women become wives, it's a whole different ballgame, and mostly a ballgame of misery.
- After some more of this kind of talk, Orlando says he must leave for two hours to attend

Duke Senior at dinner. He promises not to be a minute late on his return (or Ganymede will have his head), and Orlando is off.
- Celia, meanwhile, has watched this whole exchange with some bewilderment. She scolds Rosalind, who allowed her "Ganymede" character to be so critical and harsh of the female sex with very little attention to the fact that Rosalind is *actually* a woman herself. Rosalind glosses over it and then proclaims she is really, *really* in love. A lot. Really.

Act IV, Scene ii

- Jaques and the lords are back at the forest, and because all of the talking in the play needs to be broken up by something, there's a musical interlude.
- Jaques suggests that the guy who killed the deer during the recent hunt should put the deer antlers on his head and be presented to the Duke (!). They agree (!!), and sing about this tradition of "the lusty horn," passed down from generation to generation of hunters.

Act IV, Scene iii

- Rosalind and Celia ponder over Orlando, who hasn't shown up yet.
- Silvius enters, bearing the letter from Phebe for "Ganymede."
- Rosalind reads the thing and is shocked by the contents, wherein Phebe declares she will not love him (Ganymede). This is great news, as Ganymede didn't want to be loved, especially by another woman, so at least everyone's on the same page.
- Rosalind accuses Silvius of writing the letter because it's so bold. (This is especially interesting, as of course Rosalind is actually a woman, and her whole parading as a man in the forest is pretty bold too.)
- In the letter, Phebe confesses that she at first fell in love with Ganymede while he scorned her. Worst of all, Phebe writes that Ganymede can send his response to her through Silvius. Silvius, who loves Phebe dearly, will tell Phebe whether another man accepts or scorns her offered love.
- Rosalind, thinking of some way out of this idiocy, tells Silvius to give Phebe some instructions: if Phebe loves Ganymede, then Ganymede commands her to love Silvius. If she won't do that, then Ganymede won't take her unless Silvius convinces him to take her. Um…OK.
- Silvius leaves with the news, probably with a confused expression somewhere on par with Keanu Reeves at the end of *Matrix Reloaded*.
- Then Oliver, Orlando's older brother, randomly shows up in the forest.
- Oliver has been trying to find these two in particular, and recognizes Rosalind/Ganymede by the description of a "fair boy of female favor" with a short sister. Oliver brings greetings from Orlando, and also a bloody napkin (handkerchief) to the youth that Orlando calls "Rosalind." Naturally, Rosalind looks for an explanation, and boy (or girl), does she ever get one.
- Here begins Oliver's story of Orlando's afternoon. Orlando left Ganymede and discovered

a ragged man sleeping under an oak. A green-gold snake was wrapped around the man's neck, ready to bite him in the mouth. Fortunately, when the snake saw Orlando, it got scared and slipped away under a bush.

- Conveniently, a hungry lioness was waiting under that same bush for that same man to wake up. Orlando approached the sleeping man, who he discovered was his older brother, Oliver. Imagine that.
- Celia and Rosalind chime in that they've heard stories of how awful that brother was, and Oliver continues that Orlando twice turned his back, but just couldn't bring himself to leave his wicked brother. Instead, Orlando fought the lioness.
- Now, Oliver admits that he is the wicked brother in the story. He says he's undergone a conversion, meaning that since Orlando has risked his own life to save Oliver twice, he no longer feels like murdering his own flesh and blood.
- Anyway, Oliver talks to Ganymede and Celia with the glow of a man who's received a second chance in life. Everything is great, except that Orlando didn't fare so well and fainted from a wound he received while fighting the lioness.
- The upshot of the whole deal is that Orlando told Oliver to give Ganymede the bloody handkerchief by way of explanation.
- Rosalind, on hearing this whole story, swoons. As she recovers, she remembers her masculine disguise, and that men aren't really supposed to swoon.
- Oliver, ever the sensitive bloke, chides "Ganymede" for lacking a man's heart. Rosalind then laughs it off, saying she did a good job of acting like a woman there, which was part of her master plan, ho ho ho.
- Oliver doesn't buy it, and recommends next time the boy pretends, he should pretend to be a man. (Snarky, or uniquely perceptive among those in the forest. Your call.)
- Celia, concerned with all the fainting, tries to get Rosalind home. Rosalind is trying to keep from blowing her cover by insisting that Oliver tell his brother about how well "Ganymede" pretended.

Act V, Scene i

- Touchstone confers with Audrey, and mentions that supposedly there exists a young man in the forest who loves her. Audrey confirms. This youth (William) does indeed exist, and to demonstrate as much, the young man wanders up at just that moment. Touchstone chats with him about his background, wisdom, and learning.
- Then, in the same sweet and equivocating tones, Touchstone suggests, in both language of the forest and the court, that William get lost or Touchstone will kill him.
- William is off, with a hearty "God rest you merry, sir."
- With that potential plot-disruption out of the way, Corin is free to enter and announce to Touchstone that Ganymede and Aliena want him immediately. As in, now.

Act V, Scene ii

- Now conferring in the forest with Orlando, Oliver shares some surprising news with his brother; he has fallen in love with "Aliena," and she with him, even though they just met that afternoon. Oliver has decided to give their father's estate to Orlando, so he can live as a shepherd with Aliena.
- Orlando's a bit taken aback, but two-minute-love is nothing new, so he agrees that if they love each other, they might as well get married tomorrow. Why take a few days to think about a life-altering decision?
- Rosalind, still disguised as Ganymede, enters. Oliver leaves him/her alone with Orlando. Rosalind pretends at being Ganymede some more, and they begin to talk of the craziness that is their "siblings'" sudden love.
- Orlando admits he's happy for his brother's happiness, but that Rosalind's absence will weigh on him heavily, especially tomorrow when everyone's getting married and he's the odd-bachelor out.
- Ganymede's play acting just won't cut it anymore, so Rosalind/Ganymede makes a solid proposition. Ganymede stammers about in regards to his intention, his having a magician friend, and his knowledge of Rosalind's fortune, but eventually he just gets to the point and promises that tomorrow, Orlando will marry his Rosalind, if he'll have her.
- Silvius and Phebe come in next, and what follows is a series of serious declarations made ridiculous by the fact that they're happening in one of Shakespeare's comedies.
- Phebe is upset at Ganymede for showing Silvius her love letter, and she asks Silvius to tell this Ganymede what it is to really love. Then there's a round-like refrain, in which Silvius declares his love for Phebe, Phebe declares her love for Ganymede, Orlando declares his love for Rosalind, and Ganymede declares his love for "no woman."
- Clearly, everyone is love-struck, and Rosalind (as Ganymede) must fix everything. As for Rosalind's genius plan, well, get out your Venn diagrams here, folks – it's tricky, but it works.
- Ganymede promises a lot. To Phebe, he promises that he would love her if he could. He says if ever he married a woman, he'd marry her, and he promises he will be married tomorrow. To Orlando, Ganymede promises "I'll satisfy you, if ever I satisfied a man, and you shall be married tomorrow." To Silvius, he promises contentment, and again, marriage tomorrow.
- Then he leaves to get working.
- This would be a bind indeed if not for all the handy cross-dressing and deceit that will now finally unravel.

Act V, Scene iii

- Audrey and Touchstone are in the forest, and both look forward to getting married tomorrow, completely coincidentally. Audrey hopes that her desire to be a married woman isn't immodest.
- Two of Duke Senior's pages find them and agree to sing a little song for the occasion. They sing of two lovers, nature, and in a marvelous harmony of the two themes, love's

blossoming in the spring.
- Touchstone, ever the romantic, finds the tune badly sung and senseless. He teases that though the pages kept musical time, they've wasted his time. Zing! And he's off with Audrey.

Act V, Scene iv

- Orlando and Duke Senior confer, each professing hope that Ganymede can keep all of his promises.
- Ganymede enters, and for dramatic effect, he makes Silvius, Phebe, and Orlando repeat all their vows, which he then promises to make good on.
- As Ganymede leaves with Aliena (Celia), Orlando and Duke Senior note the resemblance between the boyish page and the girl Rosalind, which is a convenient thing to have *just noticed*.
- Now we get back to Jaques, who comments that a flood must be coming because of all the couples flowing in. (It sounds more clever in Shakespearean language, trust us. This is why summaries in the place of reading your book are a bad idea.)
- Touchstone and Audrey have arrived, and the fool bandies about this fight he just got in. He tells us all about the seven stages of lying one needs to get out of just such a fight, and it's yet another example of ridiculously meticulous courtly behavior. Basically, Touchstone, having been mocked by Jaques, is making it clear that he knows all the rules of the court – as stupid as they are.
- As they chatter, Hymen, goddess of marriage, enters with Rosalind and Celia, who are dressed as their true and feminine selves.
- Hymen clarifies everything, and then Duke Senior recognizes his daughter, Orlando recognizes his love, and Phebe recognizes that she has to marry either Silvius or a woman.
- Hymen pronounces that the four couples – Orlando and Rosalind, Oliver and Celia, Silvius and Phebe, and Touchstone and Audrey– will all be joined in marriage. A song proclaims Hymen the god of every town, as she is responsible for creating all the people in it, or at least providing the marriages so they can get to creating on their own.
- To add to the climactic action, Jaques de Boys, brother to Orlando and Oliver, rides into the weddings with some good news: Duke Frederick had raised an army, intending to murder and pillage Duke Senior's forest hideaway.
- No, that's not the good news. The good news is that just as Duke Frederick was leading that army to the forest, he stopped and had a chat with an old religious man.
- The man instantly convinced Frederick that not to murder his brother in cold blood, and to leave the courtly world and give up all his worldly possessions.
- Well, Duke Senior gets his dukedom back, which Orlando will now inherit because he's marrying into the family. Oliver also gets his land and title back, which is good. Now everyone, including Duke Senior, can return to the court and get out of that forest.
- But before they return, they agree to party like its 1599.
- Jaques, still melancholy, doesn't join the dance but goes instead to join Duke Frederick in the religious life. This is fitting, because if anyone deserves to be harassed by the

melancholy Jaques, it's the good ol' Duke Frederick.

- Everyone goes back to dancing and general merriment until they all exit, leaving only Rosalind on the stage.

Epilogue

- Rosalind admits it's strange to have a lady give the epilogue, but she assures the audience that a good play is made even better by a good epilogue.
- First, she asks the women, for the love they bear to men, to like the play as much as they will.
- Then she charges the men, for the love they bear to women, to make sure that between the men and women, the play has pleased them.
- As a final gesture, Rosalind claims "If I were a woman, I would kiss as many of you as had beards that pleas'd me, complexions that lik'd me, and breaths that I defied not." The great joke here is that in Shakespeare's time, the actor playing Rosalind wouldn't have been a woman. For the first time on this stage of gender benders, another layer is added. "Rosalind," now an openly male actor playing a female character, is sure that when he curtseys, all the guys in the crowd will applaud.
- Either they're applauding at the fact that the play has ended, at the relief that they don't have to kiss the male actor, or at the fancy that, given everything that's gone on, maybe they could.

Themes

Theme of Foolishness and Folly

As You Like It is definitely a comedy, which requires fools, but it also involves wisdom. Foolishness and folly feature highly in the dialogue, but at the same time, Shakespeare employs wisdom as a reflection of foolishness. Foolishness and wisdom can be two sides of the same coin, if flipped properly, and the whole paradox of their relation relies on that important idea stated in the play: that only a fool would think himself wise, while a wise man knows he is truly a fool. (Go Socrates.)

Questions About Foolishness and Folly

1. Do fools really have more access to the truth than others? Given the old maxim that only a wise man knows he's really a fool, is there actually any wisdom to be found in being foolish?
2. Should revered men be worried about what fools have to say against them? Does a fool's word carry any real weight?
3. Throughout the play, Jaques mocks Touchstone, yet proclaims he desires a fool's coat as

much as the next guy (who we can presume also wants a fool's coat). Is Jaques being
ironic here, or is he getting at something?
4. Are Touchstone and Jaques actually complete opposites of each other, or merely
reflections of the same condition – a tendency to extremity?

Chew on Foolishness and Folly

Jaques represents the only truly wise character in the play. He only appears foolish at times
because everyone around him is foolish and silly. He proves that he is the only sensible
character when he does not fall for all the revelry at the end, but decides to make good on the
pastoral lessons everyone else is abandoning by their return to the foolish courtly world.

Theme of Love

As You Like It ends with four marriages, so you can imagine how central love is to each of the
characters. For each pair of lovers, love means different things – Orlando loves Rosalind's face
as much as he loves her wit, Silvius suffers from traditionally romantic notions of Phebe,
Touchstone is out to get laid, and Celia and Oliver are brought together by love at first sight.
The characters all reckon with one other (and with themselves) about the nature of their own
love, and of love in general. Though love is different in kind, its spirit seems always to open up
the same path in this play: the path to contentment.

Questions About Love

1. Orlando, Rosalind, Oliver, Celia, and Phebe each fall in love at first sight. In this play, is
   love just about intuition and attraction?
2. Rosalind and Orlando don't even talk to each other properly in the one undisguised
   meeting they have before their wedding, yet their love "progresses" over the course of the
   play. Are they just in love with the idea of being in love? Is this enough?
3. When Orlando talks about Rosalind's virtues in contrast to mythical heroines, he basically
   ascribes a set of feminine ideals to her, though he has no idea whether they're true or not.
   Is Orlando guilty of idealizing Rosalind when in fact she falls pretty far in left field of gender
   norms?
4. Is it a reasonable argument that there are heavy elements of homosexual love in the play?
   How flexible are sexuality and gender here? Why does Rosalind take such delight in
   continuing to play Ganymede, even though she only needed the costume to *get* to the
   forest, not to disguise her while she was in it?

Chew on Love

As You Like It explores homosexual undertones. In Shakespeare's day, homosexuality was not
explicitly encouraged or outlawed. Any argument that there is no homosexual element at all for
Shakespeare is unfounded; the actors that would play the characters were all men, and he is
purposefully playing upon the idea of cross-dressing and flexible sexuality by adding extra

layers to the already complex fact of having a man play a heroine.

There is no homosexual element in *As You Like It*. The two main lovers fall in love with the idea of each other, not each other's physical bodies. By freeing up the problem of sexual distraction, the play becomes the pure interplay of ideas and thoughts on love.

Theme of Contrasting Regions

As You Like It is a pastoral comedy. In the simplest sense, this is because it takes place in the forest, removed from the courtly home of most of the play's characters. Yet the interaction between court and country people in the play provides some contrasts. Courtly people have to worry about treachery, and country people about snakes, but in the end, isn't it the same thing? Similarly, don't all characters, whether pastoral or courtly, have to make the same choice: to be content or unhappy? The play ruminates on the issues of being content in your environment. Is social etiquette better than natural ease? The surface meaning of the country/court divide is simply about location, but it raises the question of where people are most comfortable and free to be themselves. The difference between court and country is just a tool to get the reader thinking about the self you put on, and the self you actually are.

Questions About Contrasting Regions

1. The Forest of Arden has its fair share of hard knocks. Everyone is always talking about how cold it is, there are snakes and lionesses, and starvation seems to be a common hobby. Is it likely that this is any kind of Eden-like place?
2. The characters that have made their home in Arden with Duke Senior seem to follow his lead: they are grateful to be out of the treacherous court and in the natural forest. Why, then, do they all choose to go back at the end of the play?
3. Is Arden a magical place, following the stereotype of many pastoral plays? Does anything happen in the forest that couldn't possibly have happened outside of the forest world?

Chew on Contrasting Regions

Rosalind's transition to Ganymede in the Forest of Arden is the defining change that allows her to take action in the play and in her own life. In the new environment of the forest, she is free from the constraints of her old identity as a daughter, a noble, and a woman.

The visiting courtiers romanticize Arden in a way that can be expected, given that they are an occupying force that has been exiled from its own home. All of their magical feelings about the special bits of nature and freedom are self-consoling attempts to make do with this new and difficult life. That is why, as soon as they have the chance, they all leave again for the court.

Theme of Philosophical Viewpoints

Pondering big questions is a central indulgence in *As You Like It*. Unlike the tragedies, no one has to worry about the consequences of killing a king or lament the nature of power. Instead, the play deals with the little, everyday stuff you can stop to notice and think about. Age, love,

As You Like It
Shmoop Learning Guide

time, and the general themes of human existence are the source of pondering for these characters. Though these asides can sometimes seem random, they are interesting because we can relate to them.

Questions About Philosophical Viewpoints

1. Touchstone meets Jaques and goes off on a strange aside about the nature of time. Is the fool just searching for an opportunity to talk to people that don't know him as a fool? Is there something about being a fool that inherently precludes him from also being a philosopher?
2. Jaques seems to agree that the nature of his melancholy comes from his travels, which are the source of his learning. By definition, is committing to a life of study also committing to a life of melancholy? Is the act of philosophizing (or contemplating) an inherently melancholy act?
3. Do the philosophical asides work in conjunction with the play, or are they merely tacked on?
4. The play is definitely a comedy, and even the saddest character, Jaques, seems rather silly. Is it appropriate that philosophy be such a significant part of the play? When Shakespeare addresses philosophical concerns, like the nature of time or age, is he really being serious, or just making fun of philosophy as part of the play's general foolishness?

Chew on Philosophical Viewpoints

Shakespeare experiments with form in *As You Like It*. The romantic comedy provides only a backdrop for interesting asides on philosophical concepts that would not be central to any other story.

Philosophy is a necessary balance to all the foolishness in *As You Like It*. Philosophy saves the play from being reduced to a fluffy, meaningless piece while still allowing it to have fun.

Theme of Gender

The protagonist in *As You Like It* is a cross-dressing, courageous tomboy that goes into the woods to escape her ill-fortunes and comes out having found a lover. Gender is central to Rosalind's ability to find her lover, but also her ability to find herself. She has intimate talks with Orlando while she's pretending to be a boy (Ganymede), which simply wouldn't be allowed if she were an unmarried woman being courted by a man. Rosalind constantly reminds herself that she must be brave because she has put on a mannish disguise. As the play unfurls, we discover Rosalind as an incredibly strong woman, and our notion of her gender stops being fixed in Elizabethan norms: she doesn't have to be strong *in spite of* being a woman, but can just be strong because, well, she's strong.

Questions About Gender

1. Why does Rosalind take so easily to dressing as a man, and why does she keep up the

disguise long after it is necessary? Does Rosalind secretly or subtly resent being a woman?
2. More than once, Rosalind refuses to act womanly because she's dressed in men's clothing. If she can actually accomplish this, does that mean gender isn't inherent in an individual?
3. Rosalind is supposed to be the protective character, but Celia never really seems to need protecting. Is Celia proof that women aren't inherently weak, and that this is just Rosalind's hang-up?
4. How on earth did Orlando not notice that Ganymede was really a woman? Does he ignore this on purpose? What purpose?

Chew on Gender

Orlando is a character with a flexible sexual identity. Throughout the play he tries to prove how strong and manly he is to people that do not think so (e.g., challenging his brother, beating up Charles). At the end of the play, when Ganymede is collecting vows, there is a moment when Orlando makes a vow to "him." Orlando is up to something, and while he claims he is trying to prove his love to Rosalind, it seems he is really trying to prove something else to himself.

Rosalind is more comfortable in Ganymede's skin than her own because he frees her of sexual limitations. In reality, Ganymede's "saucy lackey" character is a real part of Rosalind.

Theme of Art and Culture

Poetry and performance thread through *As You Like It* and end up being about more than just putting on a good show. As Shakespeare reminds us, life can be considered an "art of performance" as you share the greatest suffering and triumphs with those around you. This isn't because you're playing anything up – it's because you're a human being. We share the human experience in order to understand and appreciate it – and sometimes just to get through it. While *As You Like It* features some artistic elements (dances and songs) that clearly are meant to entertain the audience, Shakespeare also considers the nuances of art that come naturally to us, such as writing poetry for a lover or singing a song to cheer a friend. Art isn't always just a mirror of life; in the best cases, it's the stuff of life itself.

Questions About Art and Culture

1. Orlando claims he posts love poems on the trees so everyone can see Rosalind's virtue. He also doesn't know Rosalind will see the poems, as he doesn't know she's in the forest. Is it just that love inspires him to shout his feelings out to strangers? Is being in love and appearing as a lovesick person an unconscious act of "performing"?
2. Shakespeare uses songs throughout the play to break up the talking and to provide spectacle. Are the songs in the play inherently pastoral and fitting, or does the play suffer from the movie-musical problem of people bursting awkwardly into song?

Chew on Art and Culture

Orlando's views of Rosalind are tied to his own insecurities about himself, as a younger brother and as a masculine man. He has to perform in order to get himself up to her standards.

Touchstone is a more effective character than Jaques because he fills a role specifically of performance. When Jaques indulges in his thoughts, it seems unnecessarily long-winded to his friends, whereas Touchstone couches his philosophy in the art of entertainment (his job), making it bearable and ultimately more interesting.

Theme of Cunning and Cleverness

As You Like It is a play where many of the characters' "getting to know you" conversations center on dancing around one others' wit. Wit is a way to gauge the intelligence of characters, but also to decide how mal-intentioned or lovable they are. Logic functions in a similar way – Orlando withstands Ganymede's arguments against marriage, and Duke Senior makes a balanced assessment of court vs. country to logic himself into the conclusion that he's happy. Wit and logic often balance each other in the play; no one is trying to come to any great conclusions directly, but by playing with words and one others' ideas, many grow to know and sometimes to love one other.

Questions About Cunning and Cleverness

1. What is the interaction between wit and logic in *As You Like It*? Do they augment or undercut each other?
2. Very little of the logic in this play is actually based on sound reasoning. Is Shakespeare making a mockery of the attempt to apply to reason to feeling? Does logic have any place in love?
3. Rosalind and Touchstone spar often, using their words to match each other. Is wit an equalizer, allowing Rosalind to move beyond gender restrictions and simply be a smart person?
4. Is being a wit just another shade of being a fool? Does wit ever accomplish anything besides muddling up a situation?
5. Touchstone claims he wouldn't know his own wit if he tripped over it, yet he constantly comments on the things he can say about the wise. Is he being purposefully self-conscious about his foolishness? Does he *actually* know or think himself to be wise?
6. Jaques philosophizes openly, whether people ask for it or not, yet he claims he doesn't boast of his thinking like Duke Senior. Does Jaques truly feel others benefit from his philosophizing, or is he just unable to keep his thoughts to himself?

Chew on Cunning and Cleverness

Rosalind and Touchstone's interaction is balanced because of their ability to spar with each other, but they are able to spar in the first place only for reasons of status. Touchstone is only a fool in the court, while Rosalind is the daughter of a Duke. Wit therefore fails as a gender equalizer in *As You Like It*.

Theme of Transformation

Transformation moves the plot along in *As You Like It*. The comfort of home is lost for the unknown of the country, transforming our heroes into refugees. Strong will and a sharp tongue aren't really befitting of a woman, but after exercising these characteristics in the freedom of the forest, Rosalind can embrace them as a transformed woman. Orlando stops being a pathetic little brother and becomes a lioness-tamer (literally and figuratively), while Touchstone transforms into the marrying kind, a potential indication that he might be able to take *something* seriously. All of the little transformations are enabled by a big transformation – that is, a change of place. When forced out of their comfort zones, people can adapt to new situations and sometimes even surprise themselves.

Questions About Transformation

1. Rosalind's second transformation at the end of the play is her move out of the character Ganymede and back to herself. Some productions of *As You Like It* have Orlando thrilled to bits to see her, and in others he's horrified to have been duped deliberately for this long, and to find out he was wooing a woman on top of it. How should Orlando react? Should he feel betrayed by Rosalind's willful deception? What hints does the text give that Shakespeare intended it one way or the other?
2. Remember that part where Touchstone appears all of a sudden with Audrey, announcing he'll marry her? Yes, so do we. Is this a significant change in the fool's behavior, or is it another one of his foolish jests to take something as marriage so lightly?
3. Celia transforms herself into "Aliena," but her decision to transform is born entirely of her own will, not out of the necessity of banishment. Is Rosalind's transformation a willing or a forced one? How else does Rosalind transform, besides donning men's clothing?
4. Oliver and Duke Frederick's great transformations both take place outside of the action of the play, though both are central to moving the plot forward. What else happens outside of the audience's gaze to encourage the other characters' transformations? Is not showing us this stuff an effective theatrical device? To what end?

Chew on Transformation

Transformation in the play is a glib event that occurs at the whim of the characters. Characters like Rosalind and Touchstone do not undergo any great personal changes, but rather their seeming "transformations" are expressions of this hidden and complex selves.

Orlando is dismayed at Rosalind's transformation from Ganymede because it reveals deep flaws in his own character, including his naiveté, gullibility, and blind romanticism.

Theme of Loyalty

As You Like It explores many different kinds of relationships: brother to brother, master to servant, leader to subject, lover to beloved, friend to friend, and more. There are certain expectations about how each of these relationships affect the characters they bind, though some of the play's central characters act outside of their bonds. Treachery infuses the play, but

so does an equal amount of loyalty. As we read the play, it's important to consider what our expectations are for certain relationships, such as loyalty between brothers as opposed to between lovers. Shakespeare gives us some "traditional" relations, but much of the action of the play is centered around the *inversion* of those relationships – it's about what happens when relations are unnatural, when brother turns against brother, when lover deceives lover. Ultimately, the play relies on the question of whether these relations can be repaired and made natural again.

Questions About Loyalty

1. Do blood relatives have any ties beyond the coincidence of blood? Oliver betrays Orlando, Duke Frederick betrays Duke Senior, and only Rosalind and Celia (who aren't even siblings) love each other loyally. Are blood relations such a weak link that they're trumped by other concerns, like competition and personal gain?
2. Duke Frederick banishes Rosalind because she's her father's daughter. She insists treachery isn't hereditary, and anyway her father isn't a traitor. If Rosalind didn't leave her uncle, or rebel in some way against him, would that be a betrayal of her father?
3. Where are all the mothers in this play? How would their presence change everyone's behavior, especially in the area of loyalty?
4. Rosalind seems convinced that wooing makes people insane, and marriage makes them boring and mean to each other. What then, is the point of having relations beyond the occasional fling, and why on earth is marriage everyone's goal in *As You Like It*?

Chew on Loyalty

In *As You Like It*, competition is strongest among family members. While the men (such as Oliver and Orlando) clearly realize this, the women (such as Rosalind and Celia) don't.

By providing two examples of treacherous brothers who turned around and were later embraced by their "good" brothers, *As You Like It* extols loyalty as well as forgiveness.

Theme of Family

Family in *As You Like It* is the source of both grief and support for many of the main characters. The play touches on the fact that being related doesn't mean being loyal or loving. Further, *not* being related doesn't stop you from being loved like family. Rosalind is Celia's cousin, and though Celia loves her dearly, Rosalind's own uncle would like to see her father dead. Sometimes family means competition (as in the issue of inheritance between Orlando and Oliver), but in other times it means great comfort and loyalty (as with Celia and Rosalind's bond). As it defines the nature of relationships, both good and bad, family is an important lens through which to process much of the play's action.

Questions About Family

1. Celia at first tries to convince Rosalind not to worry about her father, and then Celia

eventually abandons her own father in favor of her best friend. Does Celia have any family loyalty?

2. Oliver admits early on that he has no reason to hate Orlando except that he's so well liked. Would there be no hatred between the two men if they weren't brothers? Is the sibling relationship an inherently competitive one?

3. Duke Senior and Duke Frederick are brothers; we don't know their history, but we do know they go afoul of each other in their later lives. Are there any hints in the relationship between Orlando and Oliver that their future relations won't be completely happy and stable? What does it mean that Oliver wants to live with Celia as a poor shepherd initially, but will happily return to the court life once he hears he has his land back?

4. What do you make of Adam's relationship to Orlando? Does Orlando treat Adam like a generous and dutiful servant or like a father figure or like a child to protect and feed?

Chew on Family

As You Like It is full of examples supporting the idea that everyone is their brother's keeper. The brothers that harm their own brothers pay for it or repent in the end, realizing that duty to family is more important than personal aspirations.

Friends are family that you choose. Neither Rosalind nor Celia has any relatives that they feel beholden or tied to; they become a complete unit in the forest. Their bond is greater than that of cousins – it is the bond of life-long friendship.

Foolishness and Folly Quotes

TOUCHSTONE
By my knavery, if I had it, then I were. But if you
swear by that that not, you are not forsworn; no more was this
knight, swearing by his honour, for he never had any; or if he
had, he had sworn it away before ever he saw those pancackes or
that mustard. (1.2.75)

Thought: It seemed that Touchstone was talking nonsense about the knight, but he makes the point that you cannot be accused of lying if you swear on your honor and then it turns out you do not have any honor. Of course, if you would swear by what you do not have, you are dishonorable to begin with. Sigh.

TOUCHSTONE
The more pity that fools may not speak wisely what wise men do foolishly. (1.2.86)

Thought: Touchstone sets up a dichotomy for the rest of the play: in the court, fools' words have no merit, but sometimes fools are best able to comment on what is really going on (think of *King Lear*).

JAQUES
O that I were a fool!
I am ambitious for a motley coat.
DUKE SENIOR
Thou shalt have one.
JAQUES
It is my only suit,
Provided that you weed your better judgments
Of all opinion that grows rank in them
That I am wise. (2.7.42)

Thought: Jaques suggests that he deserves the motley coat of a fool, though he thinks himself wise. He admits foolishness and wisdom are reflections of each other, or two sides of the same coin.

JAQUES
He that a fool doth very wisely hit
Doth very foolishly, although he smart,
Not to seem senseless of the bob; if not,
The wise man's folly is anatomiz'd
Even by the squand'ring glances of the fool.
Invest me in my motley; give me leave
To speak my mind, and I will through and through
Cleanse the foul body of th' infected world,
If they will patiently receive my medicine. (2.7.53)

Thought: A fool is the best means to reveal the foolishness of the wise.

JAQUES
Good my lord, bid him welcome. This is the motley-minded gentleman that I have so often met in the forest. He hath been a courtier, he swears.
TOUCHSTONE
If any man doubt that, let him put me to my purgation. I have trod a measure; I have flatt'red a lady; I have been politic with my friend, smooth with mine enemy; I have undone three tailors; I have had four quarrels, and like to have fought one. (5.4.40)

Thought: Jaques means to make Touchstone appear ridiculous here, but just as Touchstone claimed, the words of the fool make the "wise" seem foolish. Jaques would like to boast that he is of a higher status than this fool, who could not possibly come from court. Touchstone gets him back nicely – he at once says he has been to court, and points out that the court Jaques so

values is full of lying, lechery, and the kind of ignoble stuff that is the exact opposite of what Jaques claims to stand for.

Love Quotes

ROSALIND
From henceforth I will, coz, and devise sports.
Let me see; what think you of falling in love?
CELIA
Marry, I prithee, do, to make sport withal; but love no man
in good earnest, nor no further in sport neither than with safety
of a pure blush thou mayst in honour come off again. (1.2.24)

Thought: It is telling that love is the first thing that comes to Rosalind's mind when thinking of activities that are inherently stupid and fun.

ROSALIND
Then there were two cousins laid up, when the one should be lam'd with reasons and the other mad without any.
CELIA
But is all this for your father?
ROSALIND
No, some of it is for my child's father. O, how full of briers is this working-day world! (1.3.7)

Thought: Love is a madness that works quickly. Even if you know how foolish it is to be in love, you are not immune to its snares.

CORIN
That is the way to make her scorn you still.
SILVIUS
O Corin, that thou knew'st how I do love her! (2.4.22)

Thought: Apparently, love is unnecessarily complicated – even in Shakespeare's day.

TOUCHSTONE
And I mine. I remember, when I was in love, I broke my sword upon a stone, and bid him take that for coming a-night to Jane Smile; and I remember the kissing of her batler, and the cow's dugs that her pretty chopt hands had milk'd; and I remember the wooing of peascod instead of her; from whom I took two cods, and giving her them again, said with weeping tears 'Wear these for my sake.' (2.4.46)

Thought: Touchstone is, as usual, thinking dirty thoughts. Even with all the sword and cow's breast talk in here, it gets worse. The peascod, or peapod, was sometimes used in country courting as a good luck charm – you gave it to a girl, and if she wore it, then better luck for you. Touchstone says he separated from their pod (or casing) two cods. This might be a silly mistake of the tongue, except cods reference the codpiece, or the Elizabethan name of the fabric flap covering a man's crotch. So Touchstone pulls two members of the codpiece away from their pod, all to give to the woman he loves. The moral of the story is, love and lust sometimes look alike, and are often the same thing, especially when codpieces are involved.

ORLANDO
Hang there, my verse, in witness of my love;
And thou, thrice-crowned Queen of Night, survey
With thy chaste eye, from thy pale sphere above,
Thy huntress' name that my full life doth sway.
O Rosalind! these trees shall be my books,
And in their barks my thoughts I'll character,
That every eye which in this forest looks
Shall see thy virtue witness'd every where.
Run, run, Orlando; carve on every tree,
The fair, the chaste, and unexpressive she. (3.2.1)

Thought: Does love need to be "witnessed," or is it one of those things better kept to ourselves (at least for everyone else's sake)? If an idiot falls in love in the forest, and there's no one there, does anyone care?

[CELIA reading Orlando's love poem to Rosalind]
Therefore heaven Nature charg'd
That one body should be fill'd
With all graces wide-enlarg'd.
Nature presently distill'd
Helen's cheek, but not her heart,
Cleopatra's majesty,
Atalanta's better part,
Sad Lucretia's modesty.
Thus Rosalind of many parts
By heavenly synod was devis'd,
Of many faces, eyes, and hearts,
To have the touches dearest priz'd.
Heaven would that she these gifts should have,
And I to live and die her slave. (3.2.141)

Thought: This is a little reminiscent of Ferdinand's speech to Miranda in *The Tempest*, in which he says he has been around the block and no one displeases him less than Miranda, though individual women have had their assets.

ROSALIND

Alas the day! what shall I do with my doublet and hose?
What did he when thou saw'st him? What said he? How look'd he?
Wherein went he? What makes he here? Did he ask for me? Where
remains he? How parted he with thee? And when shalt thou see him again? Answer me in one
word. (3.2.219)

Thought: Even Rosalind, usually a calm and collected girl, is laid flat by love. There doesn't seem to be much hope for even the most resistant of us. Is it realistic for a character as guarded and cynical as Rosalind to fall victim to love so easily? Does she have any concern about protecting herself in this affair?

ROSALIND

Love is merely a madness; and, I tell you, deserves as
well a dark house and a whip as madmen do; and the reason why
they are not so punish'd and cured is that the lunacy is so
ordinary that the whippers are in love too. (3.2.400)

Thought: Rosalind really does believe love is a madness; she is not just speaking in jest here. One of her intricacies as a character is to admit that love is madness and still be perfectly happy to get caught up in it (something someone like Jaques could not do).

ORLANDO

Is't possible that on so little acquaintance you should
like her? that but seeing you should love her? and loving woo?
and, wooing, she should grant? and will you persever to enjoy her? (5.2.1)

Thought: Only when Orlando is an outsider to a love affair can he see how strange it is to fall in love so fast and so hard. Love destroys objectivity about your own love, but not the love of others. Still, while Orlando is a little curious about Oliver's sudden love, he never makes the genius leap to examine his own relationship with Rosalind.

Contrasting Regions Quotes

CHARLES

They say he is already in the Forest of Arden, and a many
merry men with him; and there they live like the old Robin Hood
of England. They say many young gentlemen flock to him every day, and fleet the time
carelessly, as they did in the golden world. (1.1.114)

Thought: Charles implies that the forest is an Eden-like paradise by comparing it with the golden world. The court, though it is more civilized, has its own failings when compared to the freedom of the forest.

DUKE SENIOR
Now, my co-mates and brothers in exile,
Hath not old custom made this life more sweet
Than that of painted pomp? Are not these woods
More free from peril than the envious court?
Here feel we not the penalty of Adam,
The seasons' difference; as the icy fang
And churlish chiding of the winter's wind,
Which when it bites and blows upon my body,
Even till I shrink with cold, I smile and say
'This is no flattery; these are counsellors
That feelingly persuade me what I am.' (2.1.1)

Thought: Duke Senior seems genuinely happy out of the court, especially as it was a source of such pain and treachery to him. He likens the forest to a place where they do not suffer Adam's penalty after the Fall, providing the initial sense that Arden has some Edenic qualities.

TOUCHSTONE
Ay, now am I in Arden; the more fool I; when I was at
home I was in a better place; but travellers must be content. (2.4.16)

Thought: Even though he would be free of that official title "Fool" in the forest, Touchstone has already decided the court is superior. He plays at the idea that he is made even more foolish by coming to the country, and so perhaps he is destined to be a fool wherever he goes. You can take the fool out of the court, but you cannot take the court out of the courtly.

SONG
[All together here]
Who doth ambition shun,
And loves to live i' th' sun,
Seeking the food he eats,
And pleas'd with what he gets,
Come hither, come hither, come hither.
Here shall he see
No enemy
But winter and rough weather. (2.5.38)

Thought: The courtiers that have left the court are singing here. By nature of their experience, they cast the forest as the opposite of the court. The court is a place where ambitious people do not see the sun, must watch their backs for enemies, and are never satisfied. In contrast, in the forest, people can live in the sunshine, bear no enemies other than foul weather, and find true contentment.

JAQUES
I'll give you a verse to this note that I made yesterday in
despite of my invention.
AMIENS
And I'll sing it.
JAQUES
Thus it goes:
If it do come to pass
That any man turn ass,
Leaving his wealth and ease
A stubborn will to please,
Ducdame, ducdame, ducdame;
Here shall he see
Gross fools as he,
An if he will come to me. (2.5.50)

Thought: Jaques points out the failings of the pastoral ideal. Still, he notes that anyone who came to seek this ideal in the forest would find him there, too. Do we think Jaques once believed in this ideal? Could Jaques possibly not be dead inside?

ORLANDO
Speak you so gently? Pardon me, I pray you;
I thought that all things had been savage here,
And therefore put I on the countenance
Of stern commandment. (2.7.106)

Thought: Orlando assumes everything in the forest is brutal, so he tries to be brutal too. He means to contrast the court to the forest, but the irony is that the court has proved more brutal to him than the forest could ever be.

CORIN
No more but that I know the more one sickens the worse at
ease he is; and that he that wants money, means, and content, is
without three good friends; that the property of rain is to wet,
and fire to burn; that good pasture makes fat sheep; and that a
great cause of the night is lack of the sun; that he that hath
learned no wit by nature nor art may complain of good breeding,
or comes of a very dull kindred.
TOUCHSTONE
Such a one is a natural philosopher. (3.2.23)

Thought: Corin expresses the pastoral ideals of simplicity in a life at harmony with nature. Touchstone's deliberate answer is nowhere near as beautiful or profound as Corin's. The fool's answer illustrates the ornate irony of the court, which is not as great as the simple lushness of natural living.

CORIN
Not a whit, Touchstone. Those that are good manners at the
court are as ridiculous in the country as the behaviour of the
country is most mockable at the court. You told me you salute not at the court, but you kiss your
hands; that courtesy would be
uncleanly if courtiers were shepherds.
TOUCHSTONE
Instance, briefly; come, instance.
CORIN
Why, we are still handling our ewes; and their fells, you
know, are greasy.
TOUCHSTONE
Why, do not your courtier's hands sweat? And is not the grease of a mutton as wholesome as
the sweat of a man? Shallow, shallow. A better instance, I say; come.
CORIN
Besides, our hands are hard.
TOUCHSTONE
Your lips will feel them the sooner. Shallow again. A more sounder instance; come.
CORIN
And they are often tarr'd over with the surgery of our
sheep; and would you have us kiss tar? The courtier's hands are
perfum'd with civet.
TOUCHSTONE
Most shallow man! thou worm's meat in respect of a good piece of flesh indeed! Learn of the
wise, and perpend: civet is of a baser birth than tar- the very uncleanly flux of a cat. Mend
the instance, shepherd.
CORIN
You have too courtly a wit for me; I'll rest. (3.2.45)

Thought: Corin argues that the attitudes and social conventions of the court have no place in
the country, as they are uncommon and unnecessary to country living. Touchstone's wit and
his desire to be contrary get the better of him here; he uses the usual contrast between court
and country, but ends up pointing out that one is not necessarily better than the other – a
central motif of the play.

Philosophical Viewpoints Quotes
ORLANDO
…But let your fair eyes and gentle wishes go
with me to my trial; wherein if I be foil'd there is but one
sham'd that was never gracious; if kill'd, but one dead that is
willing to be so. I shall do my friends no wrong, for I have none
to lament me; the world no injury, for in it I have nothing; only
in the world I fill up a place, which may be better supplied when

I have made it empty. (1.2.185)

Thought: Orlando's anger has changed to gentle despair. By the philosophical wonderings of the worth of his own life, he has come to the conclusion that his life is worth nothing.

CELIA
Now go we in content
To liberty, and not to banishment. (1.3.137)

Thought: Celia's life philosophy leans towards the glass-half-full side. Sometimes all you need is a little perspective, which has the power to change the entire feel of what could otherwise be a bad situation.

FIRST LORD
O, yes, into a thousand similes.
First, for his weeping into the needless stream:
'Poor deer,' quoth he 'thou mak'st a testament
As worldlings do, giving thy sum of more
To that which had too much.' Then, being there alone,
Left and abandoned of his velvet friends:
''Tis right'; quoth he 'thus misery doth part
The flux of company.' Anon, a careless herd,
Full of the pasture, jumps along by him
And never stays to greet him. 'Ay,' quoth Jaques
'Sweep on, you fat and greasy citizens;
'Tis just the fashion. Wherefore do you look
Upon that poor and broken bankrupt there?'
Thus most invectively he pierceth through
The body of the country, city, court,
Yea, and of this our life; swearing that we
Are mere usurpers, tyrants, and what's worse,
To fright the animals, and to kill them up
In their assign'd and native dwelling-place. (1.4.45)

Thought: Drama undercuts even the most reputable philosophical inquiries. The serious pursuit of philosophy requires that it be more a thinking and rational pursuit than one inspired by (or tainted by) feelings.

ADAM
From seventeen years till now almost four-score
Here lived I, but now live here no more.
At seventeen years many their fortunes seek,
But at fourscore it is too late a week;
Yet fortune cannot recompense me better

Than to die well and not my master's debtor. (2.3.71)

Thought: Adam has lived a life of servitude, but sees himself as one who should not owe anything to anyone at the end of his life. He should instead be free – from debt and any other metaphorical restrictions. Adam's personal state as a servant does not condemn his philosophy to that of a servant.

JAQUES
Well then, if ever I thank any man, I'll thank you; but
that they call compliment is like th' encounter of two dog-apes;
and when a man thanks me heartily, methinks have given him a
penny, and he renders me the beggarly thanks. Come, sing; and you that will not, hold your
tongues. (2.5.25)

Thought: Jaques philosophizes on the nature of thanks and compliments. His outlook on compliments being beggarly (in that they are too profuse and lowly) probably stems from his own inability to see anything worth being grateful for.

JAQUES
telling Touchstone's philosophizing on time:
[Touchstone, the fool] Says very wisely, 'It is ten o'clock;
Thus we may see,' quoth he, 'how the world wags;
'Tis but an hour ago since it was nine;
And after one hour more 'twill be eleven;
And so, from hour to hour, we ripe and ripe,
And then, from hour to hour, we rot and rot;
And thereby hangs a tale.' (2.7.22)

Thought: This is a decidedly simplistic view of the march of time, but can you sense the hint of Macbeth's "Tomorrow and tomorrow and tomorrow creeps in this petty pace from day to day"?

Most friendship is feigning, most loving mere folly.
Then, heigh-ho, the holly!
This life is most jolly. (2.7.181)

Thought: If this is the nature of life, then there is no reason in railing against it. At least we know what we are up against, and we might as well be happy in the face of it.

TOUCHSTONE
Truly, shepherd, in respect of itself, it is a good
life; but in respect that it is a shepherd's life, it is nought.
In respect that it is solitary, I like it very well; but in
respect that it is private, it is a very vile life. Now in

respect it is in the fields, it pleaseth me well; but in respect
it is not in the court, it is tedious. As it is a spare life,
look you, it fits my humour well; but as there is no more plenty
in it, it goes much against my stomach. Hast any philosophy in
thee, shepherd? (3.2.13)

Thought: Aside from Touchstone being deliberately opaque, it is possible he is just using his balanced perspective again. His ability as a fool, as he has already said, is to see the foolish in the seemingly wise, which extends to seeing both sides of every argument.

CORIN
Sir, I am a true labourer: I earn that I eat, get that I
wear; owe no man hate, envy no man's happiness; glad of other
men's good, content with my harm; and the greatest of my pride is to see my ewes graze and
my lambs suck. (3.2.73)

Thought: Corin's philosophy is one of natural contentment. Corin and the other "naturals" are utterly unconcerned with the frippery of the court, or with men's frippery in general.

ORLANDO
I will chide no breather in the world but myself, against
whom I know most faults. (3.2.280)

Thought: Orlando states a philosophical standard (of judging no one but himself) that seems stringent, but apparently sincere.

ROSALIND
Time travels in divers paces with divers persons. I'll tell you who Time ambles withal, who Time
trots withal, who Time gallops withal, and who he stands still withal.
ORLANDO
I prithee, who doth he trot withal?
ROSALIND
Marry, he trots hard with a young maid between the
contract of her marriage and the day it is solemniz'd; if the
interim be but a se'nnight, Time's pace is so hard that it seems
the length of seven year.
ORLANDO
Who ambles Time withal?
ROSALIND
With a priest that lacks Latin and a rich man that hath
not the gout; for the one sleeps easily because he cannot study,
and the other lives merrily because he feels no pain; the one
lacking the burden of lean and wasteful learning, the other
knowing no burden of heavy tedious penury. These Time ambles

withal.
ORLANDO
Who doth he gallop withal?
ROSALIND
With a thief to the gallows; for though he go as softly
as foot can fall, he thinks himself too soon there.
ORLANDO
Who stays it still withal?
ROSALIND
With lawyers in the vacation; for they sleep between term and term, and then they perceive not
how Time moves. (3.2.308)

Thought: It is important to remember this is the first time Rosalind is having free conference of any significance with Orlando. He doesn't have a chance to get a word in edgewise, so it's not exactly a first date, but we have to ask what Rosalind is hoping to accomplish here. Maybe she is talking too much out of nervousness, but it is much more likely that she is aiming to impress Orlando with her intelligence and thoughtfulness, since he cannot be distracted by her looks.

TOUCHSTONE
Amen. A man may, if he were of a fearful heart, stagger
in this attempt; for here we have no temple but the wood, no
assembly but horn-beasts. But what though? Courage! As horns are
odious, they are necessary. It is said: 'Many a man knows no end
of his goods.' Right! Many a man has good horns and knows no end
of them. Well, that is the dowry of his wife; 'tis none of his
own getting. Horns? Even so. Poor men alone? No, no; the noblest
deer hath them as huge as the rascal. Is the single man therefore
blessed? No; as a wall'd town is more worthier than a village, so
is the forehead of a married man more honourable than the bare
brow of a bachelor; and by how much defence is better than no
skill, by so much is horn more precious than to want. (3.3.48)

Thought: It seems even Touchstone's rakish philosophy has its limits. He is fine messing around, but like anyone else, he's afraid of being alone, which is a rather poignant moment in these ponderings. He would rather suffer the complete foolishness of his country wife than be alone with his wit.

ROSALIND
They say you are a melancholy fellow.
JAQUES
I am so; I do love it better than laughing.
ROSALIND
Those that are in extremity of either are abominable
fellows, and betray themselves to every modern censure worse than drunkards. (4.1.3)

Thought: Rosalind's comment is illuminating about her own choices. It makes sense that she believes in temperance, or the middle road, as she is so deft at balancing completely opposite temperaments.

Gender Quotes

TOUCHSTONE

Thus men may grow wiser every day. It is the first time that ever I heard breaking of ribs was sport for ladies.

CELIA

Or I, I promise thee.

ROSALIND

But is there any else longs to see this broken music in
his sides? Is there yet another dotes upon rib-breaking? Shall we
see this wrestling, cousin? (1.2.137)

Thought: Rosalind is eager to see the rib-breaking wrestling match. Even before she is Ganymede, Rosalind doesn't exactly act in the way we would expect a "lady" to.

ROSALIND

Were it not better,
Because that I am more than common tall,
That I did suit me all points like a man?
A gallant curtle-axe upon my thigh,
A boar spear in my hand; and- in my heart
Lie there what hidden woman's fear there will-
We'll have a swashing and a martial outside,
As many other mannish cowards have
That do outface it with their semblances. (1.3.114)

Thought: Rosalind admits that there are many mannish cowards – dressing or "being" a man does not make a person naturally courageous. Instead, she identifies the important fact that being one gender or another does not necessarily make you one type of person or another. (Cowardice is not limited to women alone, and thus bravery might not be limited to men alone.)

ROSALIND

I could find in my heart to disgrace my man's apparel,
and to cry like a woman; but I must comfort the weaker vessel, as
doublet and hose ought to show itself courageous to petticoat;
therefore, courage, good Aliena. (2.4.4)

Thought: Rosalind has a lot of explicit assumptions about the role of women. Now she can be stronger and not cry and all of that, but it is not just because she has put on the magical clothes of manhood. Rosalind is this way naturally, but she can't express it until free from the feminine

paradigm. Still, these constraints about what it "means" to be a woman are at least partially self-imposed.

CELIA *[reading Orlando's love poem to Rosalind]*
Therefore heaven Nature charg'd
That one body should be fill'd
With all graces wide-enlarg'd.
Nature presently distill'd
Helen's cheek, but not her heart,
Cleopatra's majesty,
Atalanta's better part,
Sad Lucretia's modesty.
Thus Rosalind of many parts
By heavenly synod was devis'd,
Of many faces, eyes, and hearts,
To have the touches dearest priz'd.
Heaven would that she these gifts should have,
And I to live and die her slave. (3.2.141)

Thought: Celia says that lovers tend to make idealized pictures of their mates, and women in particular fall victim to being put on a pedestal. Orlando is guilty of the same thing; all the women he cites here have had some great tragedy or failing befall them, which illuminates their better parts significantly. Orlando's love seems to blind him to the fact that all people, even well-celebrated women, are subject to great failings.

ROSALIND
Good my complexion! dost thou think, though I am
caparison d like a man, I have a doublet and hose in my
disposition? One inch of delay more is a South Sea of discovery.
I prithee tell me who is it quickly, and speak apace. I would
thou could'st stammer, that thou mightst pour this conceal'd man out of thy mouth, as wine
comes out of narrow-mouth'd bottle- either too much at once or none at all. I prithee take the
cork out of thy mouth that I may drink thy tidings.
CELIA.
So you may put a man in your belly. (3.2.194)

Thought: Even though Rosalind is dressed like a man and puts on a man's affectations, she still has the giddiness common to women in love. Celia points out that at the rate of her excitement, she seems just as happy to hear news as to fall into bed with a lover she does not even know yet.

ROSALIND
Do you not know I am a woman? When I think, I must speak. (3.2.249)

Thought: Do things ever change? More fairly, is this statement a reasonable characterization of the feminine condition?

ORLANDO
Fair youth, I would I could make thee believe I love.
ROSALIND
Me believe it! You may as soon make her that you love
believe it; which, I warrant, she is apter to do than to confess
she does. That is one of the points in the which women still give
the lie to their consciences. (3.2.387)

Thought: Rosalind claims women are not fast to admit they are in love, though she clearly does not hide her love from anyone besides Orlando. Is this problem of being in love and not admitting it a common one? Is it a defensive mechanism? Is it particular to women?

ROSALIND
He was to imagine me his love, his mistress; and I set him every day to woo me; at which time would I, being but a moonish youth, grieve, be effeminate, changeable, longing and liking, proud, fantastical, apish, shallow, inconstant, full of tears, full of smiles; for every passion something and for no passion truly anything, as boys and women are for the most part cattle of this colour… (3.2.407)

Thought: Rosalind lumps boys and women into one category, describing them both as effeminate and stereotypically feminine. Is she suggesting that women are unrealized, imperfect, or incomplete versions of men (a position long held by many)?

CELIA
You have simply misus'd our sex in your love-prate. We must
have your doublet and hose pluck'd over your head, and show the
world what the bird hath done to her own nest. (4.1.201)

Thought: Celia calls Rosalind out on how abusive she has been towards her own gender. Rosalind (as Ganymede) seems comfortable making these statements that play up stereotypes of women, perhaps because she knows they are so far from the truth as to be absurdly funny, or perhaps because she believes them to be true and resents her own confinement?

OLIVER
Be of good cheer, youth. You a man!
You lack a man's heart.
ROSALIND

I do so, I confess it. Ah, sirrah, a body would think
this was well counterfeited. I pray you tell your brother how
well I counterfeited. Heigh-ho!
OLIVER
This was not counterfeit; there is too great testimony in
your complexion that it was a passion of earnest.
ROSALIND
Counterfeit, I assure you.
OLIVER
Well then, take a good heart and counterfeit to be a man.
ROSALIND
So I do; but, i' faith, I should have been a woman by
right. (4.3.163)

Thought: Oliver clearly suspects Ganymede is a woman. Remember, he has gotten this far by being more clever and less gullible than Orlando.

Art and Culture Quotes

JAQUES
O noble fool!
A worthy fool! Motley's the only wear. (2.7.33)

Thought: Jaques seems to make fun of the fool's fake profundity, but it is the performance of that profundity that astounds him. The fool's earnestness about his own thinking made it a believable enough act.

DUKE SENIOR
Thou seest we are not all alone unhappy:
This wide and universal theatre
Presents more woeful pageants than the scene
Wherein we play in. (2.7.136)

Thought: Performance appeals to people because it reflects their own suffering. Art in many forms reflects the human experience, and reminds people that they are not alone, at the same time putting their condition in perspective.

JAQUES
All the world's a stage,
And all the men and women merely players;
They have their exits and their entrances;
And one man in his time plays many parts,
His acts being seven ages. At first the infant,
Mewling and puking in the nurse's arms;

Then the whining school-boy, with his satchel
And shining morning face, creeping like snail
Unwillingly to school. And then the lover,
Sighing like furnace, with a woeful ballad
Made to his mistress' eyebrow. Then a soldier,
Full of strange oaths, and bearded like the pard,
Jealous in honour, sudden and quick in quarrel,
Seeking the bubble reputation
Even in the cannon's mouth. And then the justice,
In fair round belly with good capon lin'd,
With eyes severe and beard of formal cut,
Full of wise saws and modern instances;
And so he plays his part. The sixth age shifts
Into the lean and slipper'd pantaloon,
With spectacles on nose and pouch on side,
His youthful hose, well sav'd, a world too wide
For his shrunk shank; and his big manly voice,
Turning again toward childish treble, pipes
And whistles in his sound. Last scene of all,
That ends this strange eventful history,
Is second childishness and mere oblivion;
Sans teeth, sans eyes, sans taste, sans every thing. (2.7.139)

Thought: Jaques does not contend that life merely reflects art, but that life actually *is* art, its own play in seven acts. A play moves along at the direction of the writer or director, but life moves too, guided by the narrative and unceasing march of time.

ORLANDO
Hang there, my verse, in witness of my love;
And thou, thrice-crowned Queen of Night, survey
With thy chaste eye, from thy pale sphere above,
Thy huntress' name that my full life doth sway.
O Rosalind! these trees shall be my books,
And in their barks my thoughts I'll character,
That every eye which in this forest looks
Shall see thy virtue witness'd every where.
Run, run, Orlando; carve on every tree,
The fair, the chaste, and unexpressive she. (3.2.1)

Thought: "Unexpressive" here means "inexpressible." Orlando's poetry is bad for a bunch of reasons, not the least of which is that his goal is to use poetry to express the feelings that are impossible to express. Yet is that not the purpose of all art? Further, what is the reason Orlando needs to show all of this tripe to anyone that is in the forest? Do we really need to sing our love from the rooftops? Is love performative in nature, and if so, who are we trying to convince?

TOUCHSTONE
For a taste:
If a hart do lack a hind,
Let him seek out Rosalind.
If the cat will after kind,
So be sure will Rosalind.
Winter garments must be lin'd,
So must slender Rosalind.
They that reap must sheaf and bind,
Then to cart with Rosalind.
Sweetest nut hath sourest rind,
Such a nut is Rosalind.
He that sweetest rose will find
Must find love's prick and Rosalind. (3.2.100)

Thought: Touchstone means to mock Orlando's bad verse, and so employs verse of his own. The love poem, like a bad romantic comedy, can show the worst and most sickening parts of love, but does it matter if the sentiment comes from the heart?

JAQUES
I thank you for your company; but, good faith, I had as
lief have been myself alone.
ORLANDO
And so had I; but yet, for fashion sake, I thank you too
for your society.
JAQUES
God buy you; let's meet as little as we can.
ORLANDO
I do desire we may be better strangers. (3.2.253)

Thought: Though neither fellow pretends to like the other, there is a certain lexicon of courtly performance they use to state their dislike.

ROSALIND
There is none of my uncle's marks upon you; he taught me how to know a man in love; in
which cage of rushes I am sure you are not prisoner.
ORLANDO
What were his marks?
ROSALIND
A lean cheek, which you have not; a blue eye and sunken, which you have not; an
unquestionable spirit, which you have not; a beard neglected, which you have not; but I pardon
you for that, for simply your having in beard is a younger brother's revenue. Then your hose
should be ungarter'd, your bonnet unbanded, your sleeve unbutton'd, your shoe untied, and
every thing about you demonstrating a careless desolation. But you are no such man; you are
rather point-device in your accoutrements, as loving yourself than seeming the lover of any

other. (3.2.369)

Thought: The appearance Rosalind describes is not just the strange look of lovelorn Elizabethans. Most of the things she lists are physical appearances for a reason. Remember, in Shakespeare's day there was not a lot of time and technology for the "I'm so in love I'm walking across the beach surrounded by puppies and raspberry strudels" montages. Instead, there were certain stage conventions that were used by actors and understood by audiences as performative representations of feelings. The list Rosalind gives is a good description of what a character that was supposed to be in love would look like physically on an Elizabethan stage. Just think about how Hamlet looks when he is pretending to be mad with love for Ophelia – she describes him showing up in her room looking pretty much exactly like this. Shakespeare is aware that these are not realistic depictions of love; he is consciously using these acting conventions.

AUDREY
I do not know what 'poetical' is. Is it honest in deed and
word? Is it a true thing?
TOUCHSTONE
No, truly; for the truest poetry is the most feigning,
and lovers are given to poetry; and what they swear in poetry may be said as lovers they do
feign. (3.3.17)

Thought: Touchstone's claims against poetry seem another part of his general tomfoolery, but given that the most prominent poems in the play thus far have been on Orlando's love for Rosalind, it is a mean thing to say. Does Touchstone believe the youths are not really in love? Are all lovers (and poets) liars? Is this why love (and poetry) works?

CORIN
If you will see a pageant truly play'd
Between the pale complexion of true love
And the red glow of scorn and proud disdain,
Go hence a little, and I shall conduct you,
If you will mark it.
ROSALIND
O, come, let us remove!
The sight of lovers feedeth those in love.
Bring us to this sight, and you shall say
I'll prove a busy actor in their play. (3.4.52)

Thought: Rosalind does not have any business or right to meddle in the affairs of Silvius and Phebe, for the same reasons she wanted Touchstone to stay out of her affair with Orlando. More importantly, she regards this other couple's love scene as a play for her enjoyment. This suggests that Rosalind still does not take love seriously, and merely *plays* the part of a swooning heroine.

ROSALIND
No, faith, die by attorney. The poor world is almost six
thousand years old, and in all this time there was not any man
died in his own person, videlicet, in a love-cause. Troilus had
his brains dash'd out with a Grecian club; yet he did what he
could to die before, and he is one of the patterns of love.
Leander, he would have liv'd many a fair year, though Hero had
turn'd nun, if it had not been for a hot midsummer night; for,
good youth, he went but forth to wash him in the Hellespont,
and, being taken with the cramp, was drown'd; and the foolish
chroniclers of that age found it was- Hero of Sestos. But these
are all lies: men have died from time to time, and worms have
eaten them, but not for love. (4.1.94)

Thought: Rosalind uses great stories of antiquity (contemporary to the narrative poetry of Shakespeare's time) to tell the most unromantic story possible. While Rosalind jests at love here, the real meat of these stories is the tragedy of love within them.

Cunning and Cleverness Quotes
CELIA
Herein I see thou lov'st me not with the full weight that I
love thee. If my uncle, thy banished father, had banished thy
uncle, the Duke my father, so thou hadst been still with me, I
could have taught my love to take thy father for mine; so wouldst
thou, if the truth of thy love to me were so righteously temper'd
as mine is to thee. (1.2.9)

Thought: Logic rescues Celia from seeming particularly callous about her cousin's plight. Logic is inarguable, even in the face of feeling, and will probably operate this way in the play.

TOUCHSTONE
Of a certain knight that swore by his honour they were good pancakes, and swore by his honour
the mustard was naught. Now I'll stand to it, the pancakes were naught and the mustard was
good, and yet was not the knight forsworn. (1.2.63)

Thought: Again, Touchstone uses a contrary and internally twisted false logic – more akin to wit than sense. There is one of many different types of logic deployed in the play.

DUKE SENIOR
Sweet are the uses of adversity,
Which, like the toad, ugly and venomous,
Wears yet a precious jewel in his head;
And this our life, exempt from public haunt,

Finds tongues in trees, books in the running brooks,
Sermons in stones, and good in everything.
I would not change it. (2.1.12)

Thought: Duke Senior uses logic to create parallels between courtly life and country life, and concludes that the country life is one he would not change (and implicitly, that it is better). He sets up the argument by stating the court is full of corruption and flattery. In this part of his speech, he mentions all the things people might miss from the courtly life – things like conversation, books, and sermons – but he claims they can find all that stuff here. Better than that, they can see goodness in everything in the country, which he earlier asserted is not the case in court.

SILVIUS
O, thou didst then never love so heartily!
If thou rememb'rest not the slightest folly
That ever love did make thee run into,
Thou hast not lov'd;
Or if thou hast not sat as I do now,
Wearing thy hearer in thy mistress' praise,
Thou hast not lov'd;
Or if thou hast not broke from company
Abruptly, as my passion now makes me,
hast not lov'd.
O Phebe, Phebe, Phebe!
Exit Silvius (2.4.33)

Thought: Like many lovestruck young guys, Silvius is convinced that he is the only true lover that ever lived. He uses logic (by comparing others' paltry love to his enormous love) to prove that no one has loved like him. However, Silvius's comparisons are faulty and his premise impossible to prove. Yet again, reason goes awry when hit with the blind irrationality of love.

TOUCHSTONE
Truly, shepherd, in respect of itself, it is a good
life; but in respect that it is a shepherd's life, it is nought.
In respect that it is solitary, I like it very well; but in
respect that it is private, it is a very vile life. Now in
respect it is in the fields, it pleaseth me well; but in respect
it is not in the court, it is tedious. As it is a spare life,
look you, it fits my humour well; but as there is no more plenty
in it, it goes much against my stomach. Hast any philosophy in
thee, shepherd? (3.2.13)

Thought: Touchstone uses his wit to be deliberately incomprehensible to poor Corin. Also, it seems Touchstone is amusing himself as much as anybody else.

TOUCHSTONE
Why, if thou never wast at court thou never saw'st good
manners; if thou never saw'st good manners, then thy manners must
be wicked; and wickedness is sin, and sin is damnation. Thou art
in a parlous state, shepherd. (3.2.40)

Thought: Touchstone uses logic to push Corin, with his wit, all the way to hell. Logic is not really based in rational foundations here, but is used as a rhetorical tool to come to an absurd point.

CORIN
Not a whit, Touchstone. Those that are good manners at the
court are as ridiculous in the country as the behaviour of the
country is most mockable at the court. You told me you salute not
at the court, but you kiss your hands; that courtesy would be
uncleanly if courtiers were shepherds.
TOUCHSTONE
Instance, briefly; come, instance.
CORIN
Why, we are still handling our ewes; and their fells, you
know, are greasy.
TOUCHSTONE
Why, do not your courtier's hands sweat? And is not the
grease of a mutton as wholesome as the sweat of a man? Shallow,
shallow. A better instance, I say; come.
CORIN
Besides, our hands are hard.
TOUCHSTONE
Your lips will feel them the sooner. Shallow again. A
more sounder instance; come.
CORIN
And they are often tarr'd over with the surgery of our
sheep; and would you have us kiss tar? The courtier's hands are
perfum'd with civet.
TOUCHSTONE
Most shallow man! thou worm's meat in respect of a good
piece of flesh indeed! Learn of the wise, and perpend: civet is
of a baser birth than tar- the very uncleanly flux of a cat. Mend
the instance, shepherd.
CORIN
You have too courtly a wit for me; I'll rest. (3.2.45)

Thought: Touchstone's wit outdoes itself here; he ends up using logic to prove that the court is as bad as the country, though he began by asserting the court was the source of good manners and etiquette. When Corin ends the argument by saying Touchstone's wit is too courtly, he is saying it is a refined and complex wit, yet on the other hand, it is so dressed up in its own finesse and ornamentation that it is ready to fall over into absurdity. The emperor is clothed in his own idiocy.

Transformation Quotes

ROSALIND
Were it not better,
Because that I am more than common tall,
That I did suit me all points like a man?
A gallant curtle-axe upon my thigh,
A boar spear in my hand; and- in my heart
Lie there what hidden woman's fear there will-
We'll have a swashing and a martial outside,
As many other mannish cowards have
That do outface it with their semblances. (1.3.114)

Thought: Rosalind transforms into a man by disguising her height with manly accoutrements, yet it is likely she will look the same. This transformation is not one of just outward appearances; Rosalind changes her persona.

CELIA
Something that hath a reference to my state:
No longer Celia, but Aliena. (1.3.127)

Thought: Both of Rosalind's transformations are for need – she *needs* to leave the comfort of the court, and she *must* dress as a man to protect Celia and herself on their travels to Arden. Celia's transformation, by contrast, is entirely of her own choosing. She *chooses* to be alienated from her home, and later claims that she goes not to banishment, but liberation. It is clear Celia does not take this as seriously as Rosalind.

CELIA
Are you his brother?
ROSALIND
Was't you he rescu'd?
CELIA
Was't you that did so oft contrive to kill him?
OLIVER
'Twas I; but 'tis not I. I do not shame
To tell you what I was, since my conversion
So sweetly tastes, being the thing I am. (4.3.133)

Thought: Oliver earlier admitted he treated his brother unnaturally, but this is a mighty convenient time to have a transformation, after having your life narrowly saved from ferocious wild animals by the brother you betrayed. Still, there is no talk of whether Oliver regrets his treatment of his brother, and there is certainly nothing in the way of an apology or explanation. Is thorough character development being sacrificed for plot here? Is that how everyone likes it?

ROSALIND [To DUKE]
To you I give myself, for I am yours.
[To ORLANDO] To you I give myself, for I am yours. (5.4.116)

Thought: Rosalind has now undergone the obvious transformation from a young man to a marriageable woman. The more potent transition, though, is her change from the state of freedom to some tied-down-relationships. Throughout the entire play, Rosalind has been a fairly independent woman, managing on her own with Celia. This very formal "giving over" of herself to husband and father seems a transformation – maybe even a reversion – of the lively and strong-willed, whip-tongued Rosalind we have come to know in the forest.

Loyalty Quotes
ORLANDO
Ay, better than him I am before knows me. I know you are my eldest brother; and in the gentle condition of blood, you
should so know me. The courtesy of nations allows you my better
in that you are the first-born; but the same tradition takes not
away my blood, were there twenty brothers betwixt us. (1.1.45)

Thought: Oliver gets all of their father's land under the laws of primogeniture (where all your dead parents' stuff goes to the eldest son). Still, is the tradition of "I am my brother's keeper" totally lost here? Why does Oliver seem to have no natural mercy towards his own brother?

OLIVER
I hope I shall see an end of him; for my soul, yet I know not why, hates nothing more than he. Yet he's gentle; never school'd and yet learned; full of noble device; of all sorts enchantingly beloved; and, indeed, so much in the heart of the world, and especially of my own people, who best know him, that I am altogether misprised. (1.1.164)

Thought: Oliver knows he has no reason to hate his brother, except that Orlando is (implicitly) regarded better than he is. If the two did not have that strange, innately competitive relationship of being brothers, Oliver might not hate him.

CELIA
Herein I see thou lov'st me not with the full weight that I
love thee. If my uncle, thy banished father, had banished thy

uncle, the Duke my father, so thou hadst been still with me, I
could have taught my love to take thy father for mine; so wouldst
thou, if the truth of thy love to me were so righteously temper'd
as mine is to thee. (1.2.9)

Thought: Celia values her relationship to Rosalind above all else; she would even forego her
own father for the girl (which she later does).

ORLANDO
Can I not say 'I thank you'? My better parts
Are all thrown down; and that which here stands up
Is but a quintain, a mere lifeless block.
ROSALIND
He calls us back. My pride fell with my fortunes;
I'll ask him what he would. Did you call, sir?
Sir, you have wrestled well, and overthrown
More than your enemies. (1.2.248)

Thought: Love has made a nervous wreck of both of these two normally strong characters.
What is it about love that can render even the mighty overthrown?

ROSALIND
The Duke my father lov'd his father dearly.
CELIA
Doth it therefore ensue that you should love his son dearly?
By this kind of chase I should hate him, for my father hated his
father dearly; yet I hate not Orlando.
ROSALIND
No, faith, hate him not, for my sake.
CELIA
Why should I not? Doth he not deserve well?
ROSALIND
Let me love him for that; and do you love him because I do. (1.3.29)

Thought: Celia argues that loving someone like part of your family does not mean you have to
love everyone they love. In fact, sometimes it means you have the good sense to know their
love is completely unfounded.

ORLANDO
O good old man, how well in thee appears
The constant service of the antique world,
When service sweat for duty, not for meed!
Thou art not for the fashion of these times,
Where none will sweat but for promotion,

And having that do choke their service up
Even with the having; it is not so with thee. (2.3.56)

Thought: Even faced with Adam's kindness to him (which is like that of a father), Orlando still clings to the master/servant relationship between them. Instead of praising Adam for his personal generosity or spirit, Orlando chalks Adam's goodness up to being a servant of the old school – unfailingly loyal, and doing his work for duty. Orlando seems to think Adam is simply doing his duty by giving up his hard-earned life savings.

ROSALIND
He was to imagine me his love, his mistress; and I set him every day to woo me; at which time would I, being but a moonish youth, grieve, be effeminate, changeable, longing and liking, proud, fantastical, apish, shallow, inconstant, full of tears, full of smiles; for every passion something and for no passion truly anything, as boys and women are for the most part cattle of this colour; would now like him, now loathe him; then entertain him, then forswear him; now weep for him, then spit at him; that I drave my suitor from his mad humour of love to a living humour of madness; which was, to forswear the full stream of the world and to live in a nook merely monastic. (3.2.407)

Thought: The only reason Rosalind's description of herself as a lover works is that it is a rather accurate description of what some people are like in relationships. Sure, perhaps it would drive anybody to the monastery (or nunnery), but it is a pretty constant trope in the human story – the on-again-off-again quarreling of lovers. What is this about? Why does it sometimes work, and sometimes not?

TOUCHSTONE
[Aside] I am not in the mind but I were better to be
married of him than of another; for he is not like to marry me
well; and not being well married, it will be a good excuse for me
hereafter to leave my wife. (3.3.90)

Thought: This is naughty and probably not at all a reasonable allusion, but talking about "not being well married" as an excuse to leave your wife for your own bawdy ends has some particular resonance in Shakespearean England. If you want some really saucy medieval sex gossip, you can check out the way-long and surprisingly public controversy over whether Henry VIII (Elizabeth I's dad) had married his wife, Catherine of Aragon, "in sin." Catherine had been married before to Henry's brother, which Henry claimed made his marriage to her incestuous, and therefore grounds for being able to leave her. Of course, Catherine claimed she never gained "intimate" knowledge of Husband the First, which became a sticking point in the controversy. As we all know, Henry was gaining intimate knowledge of all sorts of people in the meantime, and ditched Catherine anyway. Touchstone might be alluding to this.

CELIA
Yes; I think he is not a pick-purse nor a horse-stealer; but
for his verity in love, I do think him as concave as covered
goblet or a worm-eaten nut. (3.4.22)

Thought: Celia thinks it is clear that Orlando is not a horse-thief (thank goodness for small blessings), but she does not believe him to be true in love. Can love make liars out of honest men?

PHEBE
Sweet youth, I pray you chide a year together;
I had rather hear you chide than this man woo. (3.5.64)

Thought: Shakespeare battles with one of the universe's oldest and most impenetrable mysteries: why so many girls like jerks.

ROSALIND
Say 'a day' without the 'ever.' No, no, Orlando; men are
April when they woo, December when they wed: maids are May when
they are maids, but the sky changes when they are wives. I will
be more jealous of thee than a Barbary cock-pigeon over his hen,
more clamorous than a parrot against rain, more new-fangled than
an ape, more giddy in my desires than a monkey. I will weep for
nothing, like Diana in the fountain, and I will do that when you
are dispos'd to be merry; I will laugh like a hyen, and that when
thou are inclin'd to sleep. (4.1.146)

Thought: Rosalind says that marriage is the death knell to love, or certainly to romance. The giddy happiness of love is about the chase, so once marriage occurs, the game of pursuit is over, making for jealous wives and disappointed husbands.

OLIVER
This seen, Orlando did approach the man,
And found it was his brother, his elder brother.
CELIA
O, I have heard him speak of that same brother;
And he did render him the most unnatural
That liv'd amongst men.
OLIVER
And well he might so do,
For well I know he was unnatural.
ROSALIND
But, to Orlando: did he leave him there,
Food to the suck'd and hungry lioness?

OLIVER
Twice did he turn his back, and purpos'd so;
But kindness, nobler ever than revenge,
And nature, stronger than his just occasion,
Made him give battle to the lioness,
Who quickly fell before him; (4.3.119)

Thought: Oliver points out that Orlando tried to turn his back on his brother twice before saving him. He very particularly says Orlando was motivated by kindness and nature. Knowing what we know about Orlando as a recklessly courageous guy, it is arguable whether Oliver was saved because he is Orlando's brother, or because Orlando just would not let any person be eaten by a lioness.

Family Quotes

ORLANDO
Shall I keep your hogs, and eat husks with them? What
prodigal portion have I spent that I should come to such penury? (1.1.37)

Thought: ORLANDO
Orlando clearly references the parable of the prodigal son, which is ironic given that his brother, not he, is the problem child. Interestingly though, in both stories, the younger brother is the source of the older brother's resentment.

ORLANDO
I will not, till I please; you shall hear me. My father
charg'd you in his will to give me good education: you have
train'd me like a peasant, obscuring and hiding from me all
gentleman-like qualities. The spirit of my father grows strong in
me, and I will no longer endure it; therefore allow me such
exercises as may become a gentleman, or give me the poor
allottery my father left me by testament; with that I will go buy
my fortunes. (1.1.66)

Thought: Orlando challenges his brother on the grounds that his father's spirit grows in him. It seems an implicit insult, or at least a not-so-subtle hint, that Oliver is less a man than their father for being able to subjugate any one like this, much less his own brother.

CHARLES
O, no; for the Duke's daughter, her cousin, so loves her,
being ever from their cradles bred together, that she would have
followed her exile, or have died to stay behind her. She is at
the court, and no less beloved of her uncle than his own
daughter; and never two ladies loved as they do. (1.1.107)

Thought: The girls are cousins, but it is their nurture and upbringing together, not their blood, that explains their unbreakable connection. Would it matter whether or not the two girls were even related, if the other circumstances were the same?

OLIVER
I assure thee, and almost with tears I speak it, there is not one so young and so villainous this day living. I speak but brotherly
of him; but should I anatomize him to thee as he is, I must blush
and weep, and thou must look pale and wonder. (1.1.153)

Thought: Oliver is particularly brazen; the exaggeration of his lies exaggerates our dislike and distrust of his character.

ORLANDO
I am more proud to be Sir Rowland's son,
His youngest son- and would not change that calling
To be adopted heir to Frederick. (1.2.232)

Thought: Blood is thicker than pride, or the desire for prestige – at least among the honorable. This is particularly interesting, given that Oliver will soon tell Duke Frederick that he does not love his brother.

ADAM
But do not so. I have five hundred crowns,
The thrifty hire I sav'd under your father,
Which I did store to be my foster-nurse,
When service should in my old limbs lie lame,
And unregarded age in corners thrown.
Take that, and He that doth the ravens feed,
Yea, providently caters for the sparrow,
Be comfort to my age! Here is the gold;
All this I give you. Let me be your servant;
Though I look old, yet I am strong and lusty;
For in my youth I never did apply
Hot and rebellious liquors in my blood,
Nor did not with unbashful forehead woo
The means of weakness and debility;
Therefore my age is as a lusty winter,
Frosty, but kindly. Let me go with you;
I'll do the service of a younger man
In all your business and necessities. (2.3.38)

Thought: Adam loves Orlando because the boy carries the traits of his father, Sir Rowland. It is this love that transcends the traditional relationship of a master to a servant; Adam is like the family that Orlando lacks in his blood relations. When the "master" can no longer take care of the servant, the servant cares for him; there is much more of a paternal relationship here than one rooted in servitude. Also, think of how Orlando fends for Adam once Adam has become weak with hunger and weariness. It is like a child taking care of an aging parent, where once the parent cared for the child.

FREDERICK
Not see him since! Sir, sir, that cannot be.
But were I not the better part made mercy,
I should not seek an absent argument
Of my revenge, thou present. (3.1.1)

Thought: Sir Frederick ironically thinks himself merciful. If Oliver is truly his brother's keeper, then he's responsible for his brother's actions and could take the punishment for them. Interestingly, Oliver *is* sort of responsible for Orlando running away, as his treachery is the reason Orlando had to leave in the first place.

OLIVER
O that your Highness knew my heart in this!
I never lov'd my brother in my life.
FREDERICK
More villain thou. (3.1.12)

Thought: You know things are bad when even Duke Frederick thinks you are a villain. Is Oliver callous to think he has a friend in this other brother-hating guy, or is a reasonable assumption?

ROSALIND
I met the Duke yesterday, and had much question with him. He asked me of what parentage I was; I told him, of as good as
he; so he laugh'd and let me go. But what talk we of fathers when
there is such a man as Orlando? (3.4.39)

Thought: Rosalind, lovestruck, shows that when a person falls in love, familial ties and loyalties can quickly fade into the background.

Plot Analysis

Classic Plot Analysis

Initial Situation

Orlando and Rosalind both live in places where they are denied their rightful power.
Initially, Orlando and Rosalind are both uneasy, but they're settled in some way. Orlando knows he'd like to rebel against his brother, but he's not sure how or where he'd go. Rosalind misses her father, but has a warm "home" with her cousin.

Conflict

Banishment! Orlando runs away to the forest with Adam, while Rosalind has dressed as a man and also run off to the forest with Celia.
After winning the wrestling match, Orlando finds out from the family servant, Adam, that his brother Oliver plots his murder. Rosalind too finds her uncle much displeased after the match – he turns her out with very little explanation. Orlando and Adam head to the forest in despair, while Rosalind and Celia see their escape as liberation, not banishment. Unbeknownst to each other, Rosalind and Orlando run away to the same forest. Still, it seems all around that old lives and loves must be left behind. We have yet to see whether old lives can be repaired or reconciled within the forest.

Complication

Rosalind maintains her cross-dress to interview Orlando, who doesn't suspect her. They meet and court, sort of.
Rosalind and Celia keep it together in the forest until Orlando shows up, at which point Rosalind is giddy with the possibility that love (or a big crush) hasn't been lost to her after all. She teases Orlando while in disguise as Ganymede and gets him to woo her. She can be rash and terrible at these times, but she also begins to fall in love with Orlando more deeply. This would be great, except there's a strange tension in his courting, mostly because he thinks she's a man.

Climax

Oliver arrives with a bloody handkerchief for "Rosalind" played by Ganymede. Ganymede faints, potentially blowing his/her disguise.
And we thought Orlando was just full of youthful foolishness! Now a strange man arrives with a handkerchief full of Orlando's blood and a loving message for "Rosalind." Anybody's reaction to that would be intense – but Rosalind's is especially telling. Orlando faced immediate danger with immense bravery, forcing Rosalind to react honestly. When she faints, it's not play-acting or affectation – she realizes that Orlando is a man, not a plaything, and most importantly, that he's a man she really cares for.

Suspense

Rosalind as Ganymede promises to straighten out the impossible situation – she'll help each unhappy lover to find a perfect match.
Rosalind has to come clean to Orlando about her little farce and hopes that he will still love her.

(We feel suspense, because we don't know if he will.) She also has to please all the other characters, which won't be easy. She's got to skirt around Phebe being in love with her, lack of love between Phebe and Silvius, and the possibility that Orlando might not accept her because of her systematic lying to him for nearly all the time they've known each other. It seems that whatever way Rosalind resolves this, she'll alienate somebody. (Remember that Audrey and Touchstone and Oliver and Celia are already happy couples, which means the comedy fulfilled its happy couple requisite, so we might not get any more. GASP.)

Denouement
Rosalind arrives as her female self on the wedding day, along with Celia and Hymen. Jaques de Boys later shows up.
Thankfully, Rosalind didn't have to resolve anything. She just brought in a god to do it for her. Hymen, the goddess of marriage, casually explains everything away, and insists that everyone get married in the next few minutes. Besides, no one can refuse a god. Also Jaques, the missing de Boys brother, comes in with some other denouement-y news that the bad Duke Frederick is now good and repentant, and everyone can have their titles and wealth back upon returning to the court.

Conclusion
Everyone parties merrily, mostly; we all sit down to a hearty Epilogue.
The play could have easily ended with everyone happily ever after – but to end so would undermine the fact that the entire play has been about different ways to live and think about life. Shakespeare couldn't really end with everyone happily in love when half the play was spent mocking romance. While the dancing fools are making a happy spectacle, Jaques's departure is a little reminder that there's more than one way to skin a cat – or end a play. Shakespeare reemphasizes this in the epilogue. Depending on how it's played, the layers of Rosalind's character (and the actor that plays her) can cast a gloss – or a shadow – over the entire experience.

Booker's Seven Basic Plots Analysis: Comedy
As You Like It also has the other important element of a different kind of comedy, namely misunderstanding. Some of Shakespeare's comedies lack a direct villain, and are fueled entirely by the lunacy of some hijinks-driven mix-ups. *As You Like It* falls into this category, insofar as the villains are distant from the action (literally distant, as in out of the forest), but it's also a notable turn on the genre because the misunderstanding isn't just about mucking up – it's a calculated and deliberate misunderstanding kept alive by the protagonist, Rosalind. Therefore, the play is a blending of comedic styles.

Imprisonment
Duke Senior is banished to the forest; Rosalind lives with her mean uncle who's high on banishment; Orlando's brother Oliver would like to see him burnt alive in the house they share
Most of our main characters start off in rather compromised situations, as prisoners of their fate kept by hosts that would rather not have them. In a twist on this traditional stage, the period of unease is further extended when all are basically forced to leave these situations for the unknown. Though they were kept in prisons of a sort, they are being sent to ills they know not of. Still, as Celia comments, this banishment can really be seen as liberation, though initially it's

an upset of the relative comfort of their familiar environment.

Characters are Revealed

Orlando is prepared to kill for Adam and later fights a lioness; Rosalind dresses as a man but later faints over hearing Orlando is hurt

This process works a little differently in *As You Like It* than in other comedies. The main deceit of the play relies on the characters not really knowing one other. Rosalind must play at being Ganymede, though one could argue that Orlando learns much more about her when she's Ganymede than he would've if she was just Rosalind the whole time. When she's Rosalind, she swoons with all the usual irrationality of love, but as Ganymede she's free to have the wit and sharpness that she might not have as a lovesick girl. Yet she never loses her feminine side, which peeks through at us when she faints in front of Oliver. Our knowledge of Orlando deepens as well. We see he's not just a lovesick puppy, but can make good on his love, as he does for Adam when he threatens to kill all at the banquet, and again for his brother when he saves him from the lioness.

Finding Your Other Half

Rosalind and Orlando meet after the lioness incident; Oliver meets Celia and falls in love instantly

The game Rosalind is playing is all well and good until she has her revelation as to how much she really feels for Orlando. She meets him tenderly as Ganymede, but they have to consider the sudden love of their brother and "sister," Oliver and Celia. Prompted by this, and hearing of Orlando's sadness at watching his brother marry without having his own love, Rosalind finally resolves to set everything right by revealing herself. Orlando's definitely the guy for her, and it's time to do something about it instead of just prancing around in disguise.

Blessed Union

Marriage all around, title restoration, and everything in its right place

All the folks in love get married, though Touchstone and Audrey and Silvius and Phebe are a little more dubious as far as the reality of their romance. Either way, everybody in love gets married. Jaques de Boys rides in with the good news that Duke Frederick has changed his ways, Duke Senior can come back to his kingdom (which will become Orlando's eventually), and Oliver and Celia consequently have an estate to return to.

Three Act Plot Analysis

Act I

Rosalind and Orlando fall in love, and immediately each must flee into the woods to hide from separate threats on each of their lives. Neither knows the other is also in the woods.

Act II

After finding Orlando's love poems tacked to trees, a cross-dressed Rosalind plays a trick on her man. Act II ends with Orlando unexpectedly saving his brother's life.

Act III

Orlando misses Rosalind more than ever. She concocts a scheme to reunite with Orlando – as her female self – and simultaneously make everyone else happy, as well.

Study Questions

1. How is gender addressed in this play? Does Shakespeare suggest that gender is a fixed matter with certain definite elements? If that's the case, then how does Rosalind seem to fit so naturally into playing a boy? Is Rosalind really playing here, or just exploring another side of herself?
2. What is the nature of Orlando's masculinity? Why is he always trying to prove himself? Is that just his slighted little brother syndrome, or does it run deeper into insecurities about his own character?
3. Is Orlando's love for Rosalind, a figure whom he doesn't know but idolizes, really based on a desire for romantic love, or is she just someone to idealize? Is there actually any romance between him and Ganymede?
4. What are we really supposed to think about Touchstone? He definitely fools around a lot, but he's lovable for his rakishness and is clearly a smart guy. What's up with people covering up their best attributes by constantly making fun of themselves?
5. Shakespeare provides Arden as a pastoral setting, which usually means it has some magical element that makes the characters "transform." Yet there's no real magic in this forest. Is Shakespeare suggesting that it isn't external magic, but rather a comfortable environment that lets you be yourself?
6. Is this a romantic comedy that celebrates love, or a parody that makes fun of it? Most of the romantic characters in the play are good at poking fun at themselves and one other, though they persist in being in love. Is love a reasonable excuse for madness, and do all people experience it as that kind of irrational giddiness?

Characters

All Characters

Rosalind Character Analysis

Rosalind is the daughter of the banished Duke Senior, niece of the usurping Duke Frederick, and cousin to Duke Frederick's daughter Celia. We know Rosalind and Celia have been best friends since they were tiny, so it's no surprise that Celia will follow Rosalind out of court when she is banished. Rosalind is loyal to her cousin, and cares for her father (though she doesn't show it much), and once she's in love with Orlando, she's squarely in love. Still, she has a

sharp tongue and an even sharper wit, which she spares no one.

In this play full of contradictions, Rosalind seems the one best able to hold conflicting feelings and thoughts with perfect ease. She becomes a puppy when she dotes on Orlando, though when she gets to chat with him as Ganymede, she's brutal. Rosalind faints from love constantly, though rarely misses an opportunity to talk of love as foolish madness. She is always at the ready with some witty comment, but is giddy like a schoolgirl when she thinks of Orlando. Perhaps best of all, she looks like a woman and dresses as a man.

Besides these contrasts, Rosalind is notable for being an incredibly strong female character – one of Shakespeare's finest. Though she swoons for love, she does it with a healthy sense of making fun of herself. Her ability to balance contradictions so well shows her elegant yet pragmatic perspective on life. She's smart, sassy, cute, and ultimately the one responsible for the play spinning and wheeling the way it does. She's notable among Shakespeare's heroines for being in control of her own fate and for making literary critic Harold Bloom fall in love with her. Though she is subject to circumstance, she's willing to take matters into her own hands. Rosalind uses the special space of the forest to exercise her personal agency, rather than be "overthrown and acted upon," if you get our gist.

Rosalind Timeline and Summary

- 1.2.3: Rosalind is understandably distressed over her banished father, though Celia would like her to be all smiles.
- 1.2.15: Rosalind agrees to be happy, and she thinks of fun things for the two girls to entertain themselves with. She first mentions falling in love as good sporting fun, and not at all the kind of thing that can end in heartache, disaster, and Ben and Jerry's ice cream.
- 1.2.36: In the Nature vs. Fortune argument, Rosalind argues to Celia that Fortune's gifts to women aren't so cool, though she charges it's Nature's fault that pretty girls are dishonest, and only unattractive girls get honesty and great personality.
- 1.2.62: Rosalind jests a bit with Touchstone the fool, then excitedly stays to watch the court wrestling match between the three-time winning court wrestler and the young, inexperienced, underdog Orlando. When Rosalind meets Orlando, she goes a little soft and volunteers to ask the Duke to call off the wrestling. She says she wishes she could lend Orlando her strength, and wishes him well.
- 1.2.235: After watching Orlando deliver swift and complete humiliation to Charles, Rosalind thinks Orlando is "excellent." He's also unexpectedly not dead to boot. She is glad to hear that Orlando is the son of Sir Rowland, a friend of her father. She gives Orlando her necklace as a token. As Orlando calls the girls back, Rosalind notes her pride must've fallen with her dignity, as she does indeed come back when called. She admits that Orlando has "overthrown more than [his] enemies."
- 1.3.11: Rosalind is clearly lovesick; she says she worries not for her father, but for her child's father (talk about jumping the gun). She admits she's crazy in love.
- 1.3.45: Duke Frederick shows up and turns Rosalind out, though she points out she hasn't done anything to deserve this kind of treatment (other than be hotter than his daughter).

She argues with the Duke a little, claiming that his mistrust doesn't mean she's guilty – treason isn't inherited. Knowing she's washed up and bound for the mean streets of France, she also kicks back that her father wasn't a traitor.

- 1.3.114: As Celia hatches the plan for the two girls to run away together, Rosalind decides that she should dress as a boy, as boys are tall and so is she. This way, no one will attack them in the woods. She takes the name of Jove's page (i.e., the kid that brought him his cups). Rosalind also suggests that they bring Touchstone along for their fun, banishment road trip.

- 2.4.1: Rosalind would whine about how tired she is, but she can't have feelings because she's dressed like a man. (Apparently.) She urges "Aliena," or the cousin formerly known as Celia, to buck up. Rosalind (as Ganymede) then approaches the shepherd, Corin, and ends up buying his master's house.

- 3.2.88: Walking through the forest, Rosalind discovers, posted on the trees, poems that praise…her! She hasn't figured out who wrote them, but when Touchstone teases her, she threatens to hang him for being a meddler. She does it in puns though, which is the thing to do in Shakespeare.

- 3.2.155: Rosalind and Celia joke over how terrible the poems are. Still, it's clear Rosalind secretly enjoys the attention. When she finds out that Celia knows the poet's identity, she falls all over herself to get the information. She's even worse when she discovers that it's Orlando, and pesters Celia to find out if he still looks "freshly." Celia finds the questions come faster than she can answer them, and Rosalind replies that as she's a woman, so she can't keep her mouth shut when her brain is working.

- 3.2.299: After observing a conversation between Orlando and Jaques, Rosalind and Celia (as Ganymede and Aliena) enter. Jaques has left, so Orlando is alone to talk with them. Rosalind as Ganymede works him over. She gives him a lecture on time and, piquing his interest, begins to tell an elaborate lie about "his" background. Ganymede claims he was raised by a court uncle, who ran away from love and claimed women were generally bad news. She goes on to claim women have too many faults to list, and distracts the conversation by bringing up the recent problem of vandalism in the forest, what with some idiot declaring his love all over the trees. She claims she could fix that guy right up, if she could just get her hands on him.

- 3.2.369: When Orlando confesses that he's the victim of love and the vandalizing poet of poor verse, Ganymede challenges it, claiming that anyone so in love would look a little more disheveled than Orlando does. She then declares that no man can be in love that spends as much time looking as pretty as his date. Ultimately, Rosalind claims love is a madness to be cured by whipping, yet she offers a verbal remedy. Here Rosalind offers the plan to let Orlando come and pour affection on her while she makes him so miserable by scorning his affections that he'll be out of love in no time flat.

- 3.4.1: Rosalind is a straight mess, cooing and crying over Orlando's hair and kisses (though, mind you, she hasn't ever kissed him). She does, however, notice, that he hasn't shown up for their meeting, which is not such lover-ly behavior. Celia points out that it's probably because he isn't in love. Rosalind counters that Orlando *swore* he was in love. She is obviously not so full of sense at this point, as she says she ran into her father and joked with him for a bit before going off to do her own thing. (And no, she didn't reveal her identity.) We know where her priorities are as she sighs, "But what talk we of fathers when there is such a man as Orlando?"

- 3.5.34: Rosalind as Ganymede barges in on Silvius, who is busy trying to lie on the ground

in front of Phebe, his love who doesn't love him back. Ganymede, still a "saucy lackey," begins to abuse Phebe, saying she can't be so proud and pitiless, as she's really not so pretty. Ganymede goes on to talk about what ugly children they'd have, and encourages Phebe to take the shepherd, as no one else could possibly ever want her. Phebe, of course falls for Ganymede, who warns her not to fall in love with him.

- 4.1.3: Rosalind as Ganymede has an encounter with Jaques, who thinks Ganymede is "pretty" and would like to get to know him better. Ganymede, sharp-tongued as ever, accuses Jaques of being abominably melancholy – one extreme of temperament, no matter what the temperament, is horrible. She diagnoses him with the sadness of travelers, and says other generally unhelpful and mean things until he goes away.

- 4.1.44: Meanwhile, Orlando shows up. Rosalind as Ganymede yells at him for being late and tells him to go away – an hour late is as good as not coming at all. She says she might as well be wooed by a snail. After laying the abuse on thick, she decides to stop being mean and asks him to woo her again. She refuses him a kiss and warns that lovers only kiss when they run short of stuff to talk about. While Orlando swears he'll die if she won't love him, Rosalind goes back to being cynical. People die of all sorts of things, she says, drowning, spears, having their brains dashed out with a club, and the like, but never from love. Again, she delivers more abuse, and then she demands he marry her. After the fake marriage, she points out that women are awful once you've married them, and you can't love them forever, as they only get nastier with old age. Finally, she says a woman's wit becomes so awful that she can convince you it's sensible she's in your neighbor's bed, as perhaps she'd gone there to look for you. Shockingly, Orlando says he had better go now, as he's supposed to have dinner with the Duke. Rosalind throws a fit, telling him if he's a minute late for their next meeting that she'll be out of love with him. Remember, of course, she's having these histrionic fits while in the guise of a pretty young boy.

- 4.1.205: Rosalind gushes to Celia about how in love she is.

- 4.3.1: Rosalind complains of Orlando being late again, and is overtaken by Silvius, who brings Phebe's "loving" letter. "Ganymede" complains at some length about Phebe, as her abuses are useless since he doesn't love her. Ganymede isn't the least bit sympathetic to Phebe and says Silvius deserves no pity either, as he loves such an ungrateful woman. She sends a message with Silvius – if Phebe loves Ganymede, Ganymede demands Phebe love Silvius instead, and if Phebe refuses, then Ganymede won't have her unless Phebe takes Silvius. Matter closed.

- 4.3.94: Rosalind (as Ganymede) gets the news from Oliver about Orlando's run-in with the lioness to save his ne'er-do-well brother, which Rosalind thinks is hot. Except she's a little stressed by her would-be-lover's participation in a lioness attack, so she faints. When she comes to, she plays it off to Oliver, who might be smarter than Orlando and suspect the pretty boy is actually a woman.

- 5.2.19: Rosalind as Ganymede sees Orlando, and trips over his wound and courage. She flirts a bit before talking about how hasty Celia's affection for Oliver is, again, without irony about her own love for Orlando. On hearing that the marriage will sadden Orlando a bit, as he is without his love, she mentions that she happens to have grown up with a magician who can solve all of Orlando's woes. She promises to deliver Rosalind, and then assures Silvius and Phebe that she'll fix their matter too. She claims all their love talk is like the howling of Irish wolves against the moon (apparently worse than that of any other wolves).

- 5.4.4: Rosalind enters as Ganymede and addresses the assembled folks. She checks in with everyone that they're all still in the marrying mood, and then disappears for a bit.

- 5.4.116: She shows up again, this time as Rosalind, and gives herself to her father and Orlando, except in very different ways. She promises to give herself to no father if not Duke Senior, no husband if not Orlando, and no woman if not Phebe. (Which is, as Touchstone pointed out earlier, a big "if.")
- Epilogue: Rosalind (played by a male actor in Shakespeare's day) closes the show and asks that everyone applaud. Though she'll not beg, she promises that, if she were a woman, she'd kiss anyone in the crowd that had good breath and a solid beard. She assumes that all such people would applaud her as she left the stage, maybe out of relief at not having to make out with a male actor, maybe excited by the possibility of fun times with this adventurous gender-bender.

Orlando Character Analysis

Orlando is a little like a puppy waiting for a ball to drop. He's the son of the great Sir Rowland de Boys, the brother of the nasty tyrant Oliver, and lover of the fair maiden Rosalind. When we first meet Orlando, he knows he's angry, but doesn't know what to do about it. He vents his adolescent frustration by taking on a bigger guy in a fight, and before the fight he philosophizes on the uselessness of life. In one breath, he's ready to die as he has nothing worth living for, and in another he's found his reason to live in heavenly Rosalind. It's only after Orlando decides to run off to the forest at Adam's urging that he begins his transformation.

Still, Orlando isn't really as full a character as Rosalind. He's duped by his brother and played the fool by Ganymede, who he woos faithfully while he thinks she's a man. (This is sort of foolish even if Ganymede really *were* a man, but given the deception, it's a double scoop of folly.) One must ask whether Orlando is a good judge of character, what with all his *not* noticing the boy Ganymede is actually his girl Rosalind. But despite his fault(s), Orlando is quick to love, and once he loves, he's loyal. He's a true romantic (he hangs poems on *trees*, for Pete's sake), though he avoids seeming overly soft by beating up Charles, threatening to murder all Duke Senior's company, besting the snake, and fighting a lioness. There is no lack of virility here.

Orlando may serve as the butt of the cross-dressing joke, but he's also the epitome of masculine nobility. He saves his brother, who would've killed him, and is happy for Oliver's love even when he has no love of his own. His love is true, though his wit not as keen. All around, he's a likable and easy-going guy who might actually be able to handle and adore Rosalind.

Orlando Timeline and Summary

- 1.1.1: Orlando is hangin' with the family servant, Adam. He complains that Oliver is supposed to be in charge of making sure he (Orlando) is educated and well-bred, but instead Oliver treats him worse than the horses they keep. Orlando feels the spirit of his

father growing stronger; it makes him want to rebel against his brother, but he's not sure how.

- 1.1.30: Oliver shows up, and Orlando goes at it with him, asking what he's done to be treated so badly. Orlando admits that he's fine with Oliver getting all the land and inheritance (because he's older), but he reminds his brother not to forget that both of them have their father's blood. The two get into a little fisticuffs match, and Orlando takes Oliver by the neck. He demands that his brother allow him to learn and be treated like a gentleman, or else give him the little sum their father left for him and let him be on his merry way.

- 1.2.183: Orlando has come to challenge Charles, the court wrestler, in a match where he's clearly the underdog. Rosalind and Celia plead with Orlando not to have his skull crushed. He replies that he'd just like their good wishes, as he's happy to die, has no friends to mourn him, and plenty of nothing to fill the space he leaves behind. Orlando, not exactly Little Miss Sunshine, then kicks Charles's butt. On meeting Duke Frederick after the fight, he announces he is Sir Rowland de Boys's son. Hearing it displeases the Duke, he announces he'd rather keep his hateful name than be adopted into the Frederick family any time soon.

- 1.2.248: Orlando is reeling from the thanks of Rosalind and Celia, but more particularly, of Rosalind, who he thinks is hot. He has defeated Charles, but his nervousness gets the better of him around this girl. He asks after the girls to find out their identity, and leaves the court when Le Beau tells him the Duke is out for blood, so he should really be on his way. He leaves, announcing he definitely has a thing for Rosalind.

- 2.3.31: Adam meets Orlando on his way home from the match and informs him that Oliver plans on burning him alive in his bed once he gets home. Dismayed, Orlando asks what he can possibly do now, or where he can go. He could beg or become a highway robber, but this doesn't so much suit his lifestyle choices, and he seems resigned to become the victim of his brother's malice.

- 2.3.56: Adam cheers Orlando with the idea that they'll live on Adam's accumulated life savings (which is mighty generous of his servant). Orlando praises Adam for being a faithful, old school kind of guy, and decides they'll run off together and find some low and degrading means of employment.

- 2.6.4: Orlando gives a hearty speech to Adam, who is starving, as they trek around in the Forest of Arden. Speeches aren't as good as food, though, so Orlando sets off in search of something edible.

- 2.7.88: Orlando runs into Duke Senior's feasting party and, sword drawn, threatens to kill them if they don't give him some food, ASAP. After he is chided by Duke Senior for being a bit rude, Orlando apologizes and speaks beautifully on his need for pity, being on hard times as he is.

- 2.7.133: After everyone gets past the whole threatening-while-brandishing-a-knife thing, Orlando asks them to hold off eating for just a bit while he runs to get Adam, like a doe finding her fawn. (He said that.) Thus Orlando falls in with the merry men of the forest, and more importantly, their yummy and very edible lunch.

- 3.2.1: Once nourished, Orlando papers the forest with little poems he's written for Rosalind, of whom he can't stop thinking. He's full of bad poetry and love.

- 3.2.80: Orlando bandies about with Jaques, and they discuss how much they dislike each other. As for Orlando and his unrequited love, Jaques invites the youth to rail against Fortune for a time and have a whining session about their misery. Orlando reminds us

he's an upstanding guy when he says that he won't utter a bad word against anyone but himself, whom he knows best. If being in love is his biggest fault, he's happy about it. Still, he suggests that Jaques drown himself, which is not so nice.

- 3.2.300: Rosalind as Ganymede pounces on Orlando, and mostly leads a philosophical conversation on the nature of time, while Orlando pipes in with the occasional question. Finally he comes to the point of claiming that he's the fellow vandalizing the forest with terrible poetry. He says he can't be cured of his love, and to prove it agrees to "woo" the youth who he will pretend is Rosalind.
- 4.1.30: Orlando shows up to woo the youth Ganymede, though he is an hour late. As Rosalind goes on and on, again Orlando has just a few questions. But he does jump to the good part, which is that he'd kiss Rosalind before he talked to her. Then agrees to a mock marriage with Ganymede. After some more dithering about, Orlando takes some abuse for heading off to have dinner with Duke Senior. Despite the grief, he promises to return in two hours or so.
- 5.2.1: Orlando conferences with Oliver over the fact that he's known Aliena two minutes and would like to marry her. The irony of this situation, as Orlando couldn't even talk to Rosalind before he wanted to marry her, is lost on him. (But fortunately not on us.) Orlando then chats with Ganymede about the crazy kids Celia and Oliver, and points out that his heart is heavy to see his brother married when he himself is so deeply in love (and so deeply unsatisfied). He hears the happy news that Ganymede will find Rosalind for him, after professing his love for her.
- 5.4.3: Orlando reveals to Duke Senior that he's not sure whether Ganymede will deliver, and that he hopes so, but he fears not.
- 5.4.28: Orlando tells Duke Senior that the first time he saw Ganymede, he was sure the boy was Rosalind's little brother, yet he still bought the story of the whole forest upbringing (and didn't know he was wooing his cross-dressed lover).
- 5.4.119: Orlando is shocked and surprise to see Rosalind show up. He gets quickly to the business of marrying her.

Jaques Character Analysis

Jaques an attendant of Duke Senior's court and a guy who gets excited about being sad or anything that confirms his viewpoint that the world is a pretty sorry place. He believes that while he and the Duke both think a lot, he likes to talk about it less. The Duke must talk an awful lot, because we're rarely spared Jaques's opinion on all kinds of sadness.

Jaques brings to the play a touch of sadness and dark thoughts where most things around him are light and foolish. The youths tease about love, but Jaques seems unable to feel giddiness. Instead, he provides the more serious perspective to everything. In many ways, Jaques gives the play a grounding in reality by commenting on the other characters' silliness. To his credit, he isn't a nitpicky guy, and certainly not the type to dwell on individual failures. Rather, Jaques tracks the human failings of all of mankind. He's also special in Shakespeare's oeuvre for being the one character that doesn't get sucked into happiness via conformity at the end of the play. While everyone else is making merry at the quadruple wedding, Jaques foregoes the life of

the court to live as a learning hermit. It seems knowledge is his one true love, though it teaches him only sadness. Because of the nature of the play as a comedy, he can't be a truly tragic character, but he is comic in his ability to be so *not* comic while all this merriment is going on around him.

Jaques Timeline and Summary

- 2.5.9: We've only *heard* of Jaques until now, as the man who wept and waxed philosophic over a suffering deer. When we meet him, he is with Amiens, and begs him to keep singing the song that's jazzing his melancholy mood. Jaques hopes to avoid the Duke. He says they think as much as each other, but that he (Jaques) doesn't "boast" or talk as much as the Duke. Jaques adds a stanza to Amiens's song about a man who leaves his wealth and ease because of a will to please, probably referring to himself. Jaques ends with a chorus of "Ducdame," which he claims it is an ancient Greek call to gather fools, but is in reality just a nonsense word.
- 2.7.12: Jaques delights in meeting a fool in the forest. He finds the fool's ponderings to be, well, foolish, but is glad to find that fools are so contemplative. Jaques then announces that he wishes to be a fool himself, so that he might have the freedom to say what he will to whomever he wants. As it stands, Jaques is only a sad, wise, and silent man, but to give voice and humor to his ponderings, and to be free of the fear that these ponderings might be stupid, would be grand indeed.
- 2.7.70: Jaques qualifies himself as more than a judge of individual actions – he doesn't judge any one individual, because all have been foolish and sinful at one point or another. Jaques seems set up as an objective judge of mankind's follies.
- 2.7.139: Jaques launches into the well-known speech beginning "All the world's a stage, and all the men and women merely players." We get a healthy dose of his pessimistic view when he explains his theory of the seven ages of man. Childhood isn't beautiful, but a time to be a whining schoolboy; old age isn't a chance to gladly reflect on life, but a time to contemplate death without any of the good mortal senses. To get the full effect, though, you really need to read it for yourself.
- 3.2.253: Jaques is hanging with Orlando, who has just spent all this time writing poetry about Rosalind for the trees. Jaques is mean but funny in dealing with Orlando; neither of them like each other and neither pretends otherwise. Jaques complains of big and little things, down to not liking Rosalind's name, and he finally seizes on Orlando's unhappiness to ask whether he wouldn't like to get together and rail against the world and their collective misery. Orlando turns down that offer of a fun time, and Jaques notes that the youth's biggest fault is his being in love. This isn't a very deep fault, so Jaques doesn't find Orlando particularly interesting.
- 3.3.10: Jaques has somehow ended up with Audrey and Touchstone as the fool contrives to get married. Jaques isn't terribly supportive. He agrees to give Audrey away, but then rails on Touchstone. As he is a man of the court, Jaques doesn't see it as fitting for Touchstone to be married under a bush. Jaques here relates some of his courtly dignity, though it's a little obnoxious that he gets in the way of their marriage.
- 4.1.1: Jaques, surprisingly social, would like to get to know Ganymede better. Ganymede

doesn't have anything nice to say, and thinks Jaques's stance of being sad and silent makes him no better than a fencepost. Jaques then goes off on the different types of melancholy he's seen, and agrees with Rosalind that his particular brand of melancholy comes of being a traveler – the more you've seen of the world, the easier it is to be disappointed with it. Still, he wouldn't trade the money he gave up for the experience he's earned. (Maybe even Jaques can spot a silver lining.)

- 4.2.1: Uncharacteristically, Jaques leads everyone to celebrate the dead deer as part of a spectacle. Still, the song that is sung is fitting to Jaques's character, as it celebrates the past and tradition, which it seems Jaques has a thing for. Also, the deer is dead, which is melancholy.
- 5.4.40: Jaques gladly sees Touchstone as part of the group, and announces he's the fool that Jaques finds amusing, in a cynical sort of way. He then banters around with Touchstone. It's clear that Touchstone doesn't take himself seriously on any of the issues Jaques is all uptight about, so Jaques's meticulousness only looks more absurd.
- 5.4.180: Jaques confirms that Duke Frederick has left the pomp of the court for a religious life instead. He doesn't stay to celebrate all the weddings, but decides to go off and join Duke Frederick, thinking there's much to be heard and learned as a scholarly hermit. He gives them all his blessing, in some sort of way. His final statement is that while everyone else returns from the forest to court, he'll stay in Duke Senior's abandoned cave, to learn all the stuff they'll miss out on.

Touchstone Character Analysis

Touchstone starts off as the court fool to Duke Frederick, and ends up being Rosalind and Celia's partner-in-crime for the runaway. He serves in the play as a good dose of self-deprecating wisdom, without too much arrogance. Touchstone is most notable for his incredible ability with words; he loves to twist any argument and nitpick over any little thing. He is also in the habit of driving his listeners to frustration if they're not as sharp as he is, and goodness knows the man can belabor a point.

So Touchstone provides a few good laughs. What he says is believable and usually has something interesting beneath the surface. Touchstone's name is an explicit reference to the type of rock called a "touchstone." These dark rocks could be used to tell the purity and value of precious metals – for instance, scraping gold against the touchstone would leave a little trail of dust that one could judge as evidence of how pure or mixed (and thus how valuable) the metal was. The touchstone is not itself a valuable object, but it is able to reveal the value of metals by its comparison. Like a touchstone, the actual value of our beloved fool is in his ability to reveal the purity and goodness (or lack thereof) in others by scratching at their surface with his words and revealing what's underneath. Touchstone, like the fool in *King Lear*, is another one of Shakespeare's characters that can say wise things in an amusing way without sounding like a drone. Touchstone himself comments that he loves a good fool, and more than once talks about the wisdom of foolishness.

Perhaps the strangest thing about Touchstone is that with all his cynicism and insight into

human action, he's actually a rather jolly character. Mostly, Touchstone is a wise guy who he doesn't think he is above anybody or beyond the folly that just comes with being human. Touchstone laughs at himself as easily as he laughs at others. He's raunchy, funny, and observant, and never fails to provide a witty perspective on the serendipity and capricious madness that characterize the entire play.

Touchstone Timeline and Summary

- 1.2.63: Touchstone has just interrupted Celia and Rosalind chatting. He tells a little story about a knight who swore on honor he didn't possess, and so was not a liar, just a dishonorable man. It's a motif of sorts for our court fool. He plays on his foolishness, asking the girls to swear by their beards, and as they have no beards, perhaps he's not a knave after all.
- 1.2.86: Touchstone's foolish speech rings wise as he comments on Duke Frederick's wickedness. He laments that, sadly, fools aren't allowed to speak wisely on what wise men do foolishly, though they are capable of doing so.
- 2.4.16: Touchstone notes that though he is in Arden, he isn't transformed out of his position as a court fool – instead, he is a bigger fool here in the forest. Touchstone is content with this.
- 2.4.46: Touchstone remembers the last time he was in love, which was shady and apparently more about conquest in bed than visions of romance.
- 2.4.59: Touchstone says he wouldn't be aware of his own wit unless he tripped over it.
- 3.2.13: Corin the shepherd tries to make small talk with Touchstone, asking how he likes the country life. Touchstone refuses to give him a straight answer. Life in the country, from Touchstone's balanced perspective, isn't good or bad – it just is.
- 3.2.35: Touchstone is now definitely having fun at Corin's expense. He claims that the court is the source of good manners, which are next to godliness, so therefore anyone out of court is surely damned.
- 3.2.55: Now Touchstone really argues with Corin, claiming that the country should breed as good manners as the court (yes, he's contradicting his earlier position). He uses nitpicky logic against Corin's statements, and then harps on the fact that Corin makes his living by breeding animal.
- 3.2.96: Touchstone makes a mockery of Orlando's loving rhymes for Rosalind. He delivers his own set of rhymes about horny cats, deer in heat, nuts, and women of ill repute, comparing all of them to Rosalind. Saucy indeed.
- 3.3.1: Audrey and Touchstone cavort about with some goats, and Touchstone, shockingly, seems to have fallen for Audrey. He makes a lot of jokes that go over Audrey's head, but essentially implies he's glad she's not too bright and not too pretty.
- 3.3.38: Audrey notes that she's glad she's not a prostitute, and he praises the gods that she's ugly, as being prettier might have made her less pure. Suddenly, Touchstone brings up that he's gotten a vicar from the next village over to marry them. We're all a little shocked that he should turn out to be the marrying kind.
- 3.3.48: Touchstone gives us a funny speech about how being married isn't so bad, as the horns of a cuckold – or more colloquially, a whipped husband – are more honorable than

the bare brow of a bachelor.

- 3.3.79: Touchstone makes a string of analogies about nature: as a falcon needs a bell, so too does man have his desires. Or, more appropriate to Touchstone's case, he needs to get married because a man has needs.
- 3.3.90: Touchstone points out that getting an inexperienced village vicar to marry him and Audrey under a bush is actually a great idea, because the less formal their marriage is, the less binding, leaving him free to "marry" another maid later.
- 5.1.1: Touchstone chats up Audrey and mentions he's heard of a forest youth that also has a crush on her.
- 5.1.10: Touchstone claims meeting fools is the very sustenance of his life, and admits he can't hold himself back from making a mockery. Just then, Audrey's poor unsuspecting admirer, William, shows up. Touchstone has a series of jokes at his expense, centered around the fact that the boy says he has some fine wit himself. Touchstone then, suddenly a philosopher king, points out that only wise men know they are fools, and only fools think themselves wise men, which would have been original if Socrates hadn't already said it. He lights into poor William and eventually sends him packing, threatening to kill him if he shows his face again.
- 5.4.43: Touchstone argues to the lords assembled around Duke Senior that he is a court man, having done all the courtly things; he's danced, lied to women, betrayed his friends, chatted up his enemies, failed to pay his extraordinary bills at three tailors' places, and also backed away from every fight he started.
- 5.4.54: In chatting up the Duke, Touchstone elaborates on his desire to marry Audrey amidst the "country copulatives." She may be unattractive, but Audrey is honest (meaning chaste).
- 5.4.68: Touchstone distracts everyone from the suspense of waiting for Rosalind to show up by outlining the courtly facts of fighting. We get a long story about of the art of a quarrel. Touchstone describes in detail one particular argument he started with some fellow over the cut of the other guy's beard.
- 5.4.90: Touchstone reiterates the seven degrees of lying, and points out that any disagreement can be avoided by "equivocation" or talking around the truth. One need only put in an "if," as in "If you said that, then I said this," and the truth is as good as hidden, the fight over, and everyone happy with their share of lies. This is Touchstone's last speech in the play, so it's representative of how he thinks. As long as everyone's a bit happier, the means to happiness (and implicitly the truth) are immaterial.

Celia Character Analysis

Celia is the daughter of Duke Frederick, cousin to Rosalind, and a general balance to Rosalind's foolish love. Celia values her relationship with Rosalind so much that very little else matters to her. This makes sense, as the girls initially seem so similar. Like Rosalind, Celia is a quick wit and dismissive, preferring to mock over speaking in earnest. As the play develops, Celia is confined more and more to simply reacting to Rosalind's antics. Through Celia, we get to investigate Rosalind's changing attitude toward love, which is contrasted by Celia's unchanging skepticism. Initially, Celia and Rosalind are partners in crime, jesting together,

running off together, changing their identities together (Celia becomes Aliena), and generally having fun… together. Celia even declares their trip into the forest isn't banishment, but a chance at liberty, as they get to be the women they want to be (together). Celia and Rosalind's relationship changes once Orlando enters the scene. Celia is relegated to dealing with Rosalind's constant lovesickness and hijinks as Ganymede.

Rosalind and Celia both see love as foolish fun at the beginning of the play, but things change when the girls get to the forest and learn that Orlando is there. It turns out that even though Rosalind thinks love is foolish, she's not above being foolish herself. Celia, who is not in love, has to watch her friend embrace all the silly stuff they've spent their time mocking. In that case, it is no surprise that throughout the play Celia becomes more and more surly, perhaps disenchanted with her friend's enchantment. Like Touchstone or Rosalind, Celia delights in foolishness, but unlike the others, she seems to think even foolishness can only be fun for so long. When Celia begins to tell Rosalind that Orlando doesn't really love her, the clear divide between the cousins becomes apparent. Celia perhaps resents Rosalind's attention to Orlando, but it seems she particularly resents that her friend takes the foolishness of love seriously.

Celia's disdain of love comes into perspective when Celia herself falls for a guy. Celia's relationship with Oliver isn't a particularly deep one, but it's significant in the play because it sets off how unusual Rosalind's approach to love actually is. For all Celia's poo-pooing about love, once she finds a man we literally never hear from her again. She drops out of the play, totally enamored of her new boy. Celia then becomes a hypocrite of sorts; she loses herself in another person, and thus is lost to the world.

Rosalind may be giddy about being in love, but she's actually done a remarkable job of keeping her own identity in the process. Because she knows love is foolish, Rosalind can be in love without being a fool for love. Celia's disappearance highlights exactly what Rosalind didn't do, making Rosalind even more of an extraordinary woman. Unfortunately, Duke Frederick ends up being right – Rosalind one-ups Celia, and we all think she's a better catch than his daughter.

Celia Timeline and Summary

- 1.2.1: Celia tries to comfort Rosalind, who is bummed out about her banished father.
- 1.2.8: Celia chides Rosalind for still being grumpy about her banished father situation. Celia says she must love Rosalind more than Rosalind loves her, as Celia wouldn't be grumpy if their roles were reversed. If Celia had been left behind when her father was banished, Celia would be sure to take her uncle (Duke Senior) as her own father, so long as it meant getting to stay with Rosalind.
- 1.2.17: Celia points out that she's her father's only child, and when her father dies, Rosalind will be his heir, because whatever he takes from Rosalind, Celia will make up in her affections towards her cousin. She swears on her honor that she'll make it all up to Rosalind, and again asks Rosalind to be merry.
- 1.2.26: As the two try to distract themselves, Rosalind asks Celia what she thinks of falling

in love. Celia replies that she hopes Rosalind gives it a shot, as watching her run around at the mercy of love would be good sporting fun. Still, she warns that Rosalind shouldn't seriously love anyone, or have so much fun with them that she can't wear the youthful blush of her chastity.

- 1.2.31: Celia suggests she and Rosalind should make fun of Fortune, who she describes as a housewife spinning at her wheel. Celia notes that Fortune doesn't bestow her gifts equally on everyone.

- 1.2.37: Celia responds to Rosalind's comment that Fortune really messes up when it comes to women. Celia notes that those women who are pretty are rarely honest (also meaning chaste), while those who are chaste and honest are rarely pretty.

- 1.2.43: Rosalind argues that when discussing women's traits, Celia's actually talking about Nature's doing, not Fortune's. Celia counters that Fortune and Nature work independently, as a good-looking lady can fall into a fire – then, though she was pretty by Nature, she's made ugly by Fortune. Celia thinks Nature gives us the wit we need to rise above our fortunes. As Touchstone the fool enters the scene, Celia says his presence is the work of Fortune.

- 1.2.51: Rosalind claims Touchstone's entrance is an example of Fortune cutting off the wit granted to them by Nature. Celia says Touchstone's entrance is actually the work of Nature; the goddess must've been listening to their conversation, found that their wits were too dull to reasonably converse about the goddesses, and sent in Touchstone to sharpen their wits (as Touchstone = whetstone = a sharpening tool for dull blades).

- 1.2.68: Celia jovially teases Touchstone as he tells his silly story about the knight with no honor. Celia says she swears by her beard that Touchstone is a knave, though she has no beard. (So who is this joke really on, anyway?)

- 1.2.83: Further into this knight story, Celia asks who the knight is. Touchstone replies he's one whom her father, Duke Frederick, loves. Celia thinks this is enough to consider the knight honorable, even if he has no honor. Celia warmly tells Touchstone to bugger off, as he'll be whipped for slander one of these days.

- 1.2.88: Celia jokes some more as Touchstone laments that fools cannot comment on the actions of wise men. She says when fools are silenced, the little foolishness that wise men have seems like big foolishness (as there's no longer a frame of reference). Celia then notes Monsieur Le Beau is on his way.

- 1.2.94: Celia looks not-so-eagerly forward to Monsieur Le Beau's news, claiming he'll deliver it like a pigeon feeds their young. (Pigeons feed their young by vomiting already-chewed food into their young's mouths.)

- 1.2.101: Celia hears from Le Beau that she and Rosalind have missed out on sport, and she's all excited to hear what that sport is. As Le Beau tries to tell them about the wrestling and rib-breaking, Celia's full of jokes and mockery.

- 1.2.140: Celia agrees with Touchstone: it's the first time she's ever heard that rib-breaking was a sport for ladies. Still, she's eager to stay and watch the wrestling, which happens to be starting now, where they are standing.

- 1.2.153: Celia notes that the challenger, Orlando, looks too young to be wrestling, though he does look like a winner. (Hooray for double-meaning!) Celia tells Le Beau to call the young man over, so she and Rosalind can give him a good talking-to.

- 1.2.173: Celia entreats Orlando to give up this silly notion of fighting court-champion Charles, as Charles is so much stronger. She says if Orlando could really see Charles's strength, or know his own weakness better, then his fear would lead him to fight a more

equal guy, one with less broken ribs in his wake. Celia says she and Rosalind both wish Orlando would quit trying to fight Charles – for his own safety.

- 1.2.196: Still, as Rosalind promises her strength will go with Orlando, Celia promises the same. She wishes Orlando well, saying she hopes he gets his heart's desires. As Orlando readies to fight, Celia says if she were invisible, she'd take Charles down by the leg.

- 1.2.214: The wrestling has begun, and Celia says if she had the supernatural power to strike someone down, she knows who it would be (presumably Charles). Just then, Orlando throws down Charles (like magic!).

- 1.2.231: Everyone watches as Duke Frederick (Celia's father) refuses to praise Orlando once he finds out Orlando is the son of his dead enemy, Sir Rowland de Boys. Celia is taken aback by her father's poor behavior, and tells Rosalind if she were her father, she wouldn't act that way.

- 1.2.239: After the match, Celia encourages Rosalind to join her in thanking Orlando for the good sport and encouraging him. Given her father's harshness towards the young man, Celia feels particularly obligated to be nice. Speaking to Orlando, Celia praises him as very deserving of his win. She says if Orlando keeps his promises in love as well as he kept his promise in the fight, then his wife will be happy indeed.

- 1.2.255: Though Celia has already said her goodbyes to the gentlemen, Orlando seems to call Rosalind back. Celia asks her if she will go to Orlando.

- 1.3.1: Back at Duke Frederick's palace, Celia finds Rosalind a wreck. She asks what's going on and whether Rosalind will talk about it with her.

- 1.3.4: As Rosalind says she doesn't have a word to throw at a dog, Celia tells her that Rosalind's words are too good for dogs, but not too good for Celia. She begs to be burdened with whatever it is that's upsetting Rosalind so. Celia wonders whether all of Rosalind's laments are for her banished father.

- 1.3.13: Rosalind then says it's not her father, but her future child's father (Orlando). Celia realizes Rosalind's been infected with a major case of lovesickness. She says Rosalind's fancies are like burs (those sticky little seeds that get stuck in your clothes in the woods), and those burs can be avoided if we just stick to the path instead of wandering off into the woods (the woods being our fancies concerning love).

- 1.3.18: Celia says if these burs are in Rosalind's heart, as Rosalind claims, then she should cough them up.

- 1.3.24: Celia continues to pun about things like phlegm with Rosalind. But eventually, she gets down to earnest business. Celia wonders if it's possible that Rosalind could really fall in love so suddenly.

- 1.3.31: Celia hears Rosalind's logic that because her father and Orlando's father were good friends, Rosalind and Orlando are meant to love each other. Celia is dismissive, and points out that by Rosalind's logic, because Celia's father hated Orlando's father, Celia should hate Orlando. The logic must be faulty, because Celia doesn't hate Orlando at all.

- 1.3.36: Rosalind pleads with Celia, begging her not to hate Orlando. Celia teases back, asking if perhaps Orlando doesn't deserve to be hated after all.

- 1.3.40: Celia notes her father's eyes are full of anger as he enters the scene between herself and Rosalind.

- 1.3.66: After hearing Rosalind and her father go back and forth about banishing Rosalind, Celia steps up and asks him to listen to her.

- 1.3.69: Duke Frederick tells Celia that it was only for her sake that Rosalind wasn't initially banished along with Duke Senior (Rosalind's father). Celia speaks bravely back; she says

it wasn't her pleading, but her father's own pleasure and remorse that kept the young Rosalind from banishment. Celia says when the banishment occurred, she was too young to really value Rosalind, but since that time, the two have become inseparable. Celia claims if Rosalind is a traitor, then so is she. After all, she says, she and Rosalind have done everything together: slept, learned, played. In all ways, Celia says, she and Rosalind come as a pair.

- 1.3.85: Celia ignores her father's statement that the people will look more fondly on her once Rosalind is gone. Instead, Celia says if her father banishes Rosalind, then he also banishes her, as she cannot live without Rosalind's company.
- 1.3.90: As Duke Frederick, exits, Celia is quick to comfort Rosalind. Celia asks where Rosalind will go, and tells her that she is not to be any more grieved by Duke Frederick's rashness than Celia is herself.
- 1.3.92: Celia points out that Rosalind has no more reason to be upset than she (Celia) does. Celia comforts her cousin, saying she won't be alone – after all, Duke Frederick banished both of them by his decision.
- 1.3.96: Celia wasn't kidding about not being separated from Rosalind. Though the Duke didn't explicitly banish her, Celia says Rosalind should know that they are as good as one. From now on, Rosalind won't bear her grief alone. Duke Frederick might as well find another heir, as there's no way Rosalind's leaving without her cousin. Now it's just up to the girls to plan their escape.
- 1.3.107: Though Rosalind is at a loss for where they could go, Celia recommends that they head to the Forest of Arden to find Duke Senior (her uncle and Rosalind's father).
- 1.3.111: Rosalind worries they'll be the target of thieves, being two pretty, young girls going to the forest alone. Celia says that she'll dress up in rags and dirty her face. If Rosalind does the same, Celia thinks they'll get to the forest without being bothered by anybody. Rosalind suggests that she, who is the taller of the two, should dress like a boy, while Celia dresses like a girl.
- 1.3.123: Celia's first reaction to Rosalind's unorthodox cross-dressing idea is essentially, "So what should I call you when you're a man?" She's totally down with the plan.
- 1.3.127: Celia chooses her own name, "Aliena," which means "the estranged one" in Latin. She says this name refers to her status (presumably as an estranged person).
- 1.3.132: Celia says she'll get Touchstone to come along, no problem. For the rest of the plan, she thinks they should get their jewels and money together and take pains to conceal themselves from the people that will be surely be sent looking for them once Duke Frederick learns that his daughter has fled. Most importantly, Celia declares that their flight is actually not a punishment, but a journey to liberty.
- 2.4.9: Now in the forest, Celia asks Touchstone and Rosalind to bear with her. She's too tired to keep going on this demanding forest trek right now.
- 2.4.64: Celia says she's rather close to passing out from hunger. She asks Rosalind or Touchstone to go talk to the man they've found in the wood, who she hopes can give them food in exchange for gold.
- 3.2.125: Celia comes upon Rosalind reading a verse she found hung in a tree, which details how Rosalind manages to encompass all the best traits of all the greatest women of all time. The words rightfully belong to Orlando, but here's where the miracle of stage direction comes in. Because this is a play, Celia's character can appear skeptical, or mocking, or just plain amused as she reads this rather lovesick verse.
- 3.2.163: Celia has ushered the men away so she can talk to Rosalind privately. She asks if

Rosalind has read the poetry, and teases about how clumsy they are. Celia wonders if Rosalind can have heard the verses without asking how her name came to be hung on so many trees. Celia presses Rosalind about whether she really has no idea who wrote all these smitten poems.

- 3.2.181: Celia reminds Rosalind that the poet is actually the same man Rosalind gave her necklace to at the wrestling match.
- 3.2.184: Rosalind still doesn't quite get it, and Celia is jovially exasperated, wondering how Rosalind could possibly have not guessed that Orlando is 1) in the forest and 2) still hot for her.
- 3.2.204: Celia is naughty here; as Rosalind asks her to take the cork out of her mouth that's clearly stopping her from spilling the poet's identity, Celia counters that Rosalind would drink up Celia's words like she'd let a man into her belly.
- 3.2.208: Celia, knowing Rosalind's about to explode from curiosity, drags on the Q&A. She says the poet has only a little bit of a beard (meaning he's young) before she finally lets out that the author is none other than Orlando, the very guy who defeated Charles and conquered Rosalind's heart in world-record time.
- 3.2.225: When Rosalind finally gets it, she nearly falls over herself with excitement and rattles off ten-thousand questions about Orlando, which she asks Celia to answer all in one word. Celia laughingly says she'd need to have the largest mouth in the world to do such a thing, and that Rosalind is asking as much as a catechism.
- 3.2.232: Rosalind wants more and more details about Orlando, and Celia says it's easier to count atoms than to field all the questions a lover has about a crush. She won't answer all of Rosalind's queries, but tells her she'll give just a taste of the story of how she found Orlando – that should be enough to please the girl. Basically, she found Orlando stretched out under a tree. Celia describes him as a dropped acorn or a wounded knight. Rosalind keeps interrupting her story, until finally Celia gets exasperated and says, "Hey! There Orlando is now! Maybe you should ask *him* your eight million questions."
- 3.4.2: Celia finds Rosalind after Rosalind's first forest meeting with Orlando. Rosalind demands that Celia not talk to her, as she'll begin to cry. Celia points out, helpfully, that Rosalind can cry all she wants, but maybe she should remember that tears aren't really becoming on a man, and Rosalind is after all still supposed to be a man.
- 3.4.5: Rosalind seeks a little sympathy, and asks if she doesn't actually have good reason to cry. Celia promises her she has as good a reason to cry as she could want.
- 3.4.8: Rosalind fawns over Orlando, and Celia manages to mockingly answer each of Rosalind's praises. Rosalind loves Orlando's hair, and Celia notes it's like Judas's hair color (yes, the Judas from the Bible). Rosalind praises Orlando's kisses for being as holy as eating holy bread. Celia responds that she bets Orlando's kisses are so holy and virginal that it's like he borrowed his lips from Diana, goddess of chastity.
- 3.4.20: Celia is almost explicitly mean (or looking out for her friend, depending on your perspective). Rosalind wonders why Orlando hasn't shown up yet for their promised meeting, and Celia says, quite plainly, that he hasn't shown up because there's no truth in him (and implicitly no truth in his love for Rosalind).
- 3.4.21: Rosalind asks if Celia really thinks that. She replies that, while she does believe Orlando to be more trustworthy than the common thief, she doesn't think he's dependable in love.
- 3.4.26: Rosalind asks outright whether Celia is saying that Orlando isn't true in love. Celia replies that maybe he's true when he's in love, but she thinks he's not actually in love in

this case. (Ouch!)

- 3.4.29: Rosalind chides that Celia herself heard Orlando say he was in love, but Celia counters that "was" in love isn't "is" in love. Besides quibbling about the past and present tense, Celia says a lover can't be trusted because lovers confirm "false reckonings," or to otherwise promise the truth, even if they lie. Celia then adds that Orlando has been hanging out with Duke Senior, Rosalind's dad, in the forest.

- 3.4.40: Celia lights into Orlando again after Rosalind praises the guy some more. Celia says Orlando is ready to write brave verses, and speak brave oaths, but he breaks them just as bravely. (She plays here on the meaning of brave as both courageous, but also meaning "full of bravado," or all talk and no action.) Celia compares Orlando to an amateur jouster who can't properly direct his horse and breaks his jousting stick. Still, she says anything can seem brave, if it's undertaken by youth and guided by folly.

- 4.1.66: Orlando has finally shown up for his meeting with Rosalind (as Ganymede), and Celia teases about the whole setup. Ganymede says Orlando should call him "Rosalind," and Celia says Orlando can call Ganymede whatever he pleases, though the real Rosalind is bound to be better looking.

- 4.1.128: Rosalind (as Ganymede) is playing games with Orlando. She suggests they should have a fake marriage ceremony, and Celia should be the priest who marries them. Celia says she can't say the words to do it.

- 4.1.130: Celia, seemingly a little exasperated, relents and pretends to be a priest. Celia asks Orlando if he'll have "this Rosalind" as his wife.

- 4.1.201: After this little marriage episode, Rosalind launches into the fact that women are great when you're dating them, but that wives are a whole other type of awful. Celia listens to all of this patiently, but once Orlando leaves, she scolds Rosalind for being so critical of women, even if she is dressed up as a man. Celia says they should lift up Rosalind's manly clothes and expose her feminine body, but also expose that she's like a bird that has soiled her own nest (i.e., she's a woman that has spoken badly of her own kind).

- 4.1.211: Rosalind takes this criticism lightly, and says her affection is so deep that no one knows how deep it goes; it seems bottomless. Celia says it must *really* be bottomless, as it seems affections fall out of it as fast as they're poured in (meaning Rosalind is fickle and changing in her affections). Basically, Celia is saying Rosalind is more a leaky tube of love (with holes on both ends) than a vase.

- 4.1.218: As Rosalind says she'll lie around and sigh about Orlando, Celia won't play an accomplice to her cousin's lovesickness. Instead, she curtly announces that she's off to sleep.

- 4.3.3: Yet again, Rosalind complains that Orlando hasn't shown up for their promised meeting. Celia, not being too helpful, says Orlando must've taken his "pure love and troubled brain" and set off with his bows and arrows, not to see Rosalind, but to go to sleep.

- 4.3.65: Celia and Rosalind listen to the letter Phebe has sent to Ganymede, with Silvius as the messenger. Silvius seems really ignorant of the fact that this is a horrible thing for Phebe (his crush) to have done to him, so Celia pities him, calling him a "poor shepherd."

- 4.3.78: Celia gives Oliver, who's just entered the scene, instructions to their house. She tells him he can go there, though there's nobody home (without pointing out that she and Ganymede must be the people Oliver is looking for in the house). This is Oliver's first interaction with Celia.

- 4.3.90: Celia admits, after Oliver recognizes her and "Ganymede" by their descriptions, that they are indeed the owners of house he's looking for, though they're not boasting. As Oliver gets going about the story with him and Orlando, Celia urges him on.
- 4.3.121: Oliver (who has not yet identified himself) begins to tell about how Orlando came upon a sleeping man he realized was his elder brother. Celia then jumps in, and says she's heard Orlando talk about that brother, who is a pretty awful guy. As Oliver finally reveals his identity, Celia asks if he's the Oliver who tried to kill Orlando so often.
- 4.3.157: Rosalind faints after hearing about Orlando's lioness encounter, and Celia tends to her in a bit of a panic.
- 4.3.159: Oliver suggests a lot of people sometimes faint when they see blood, and Celia assures him that there's more to "Ganymede's" fainting than just the blood. For the first time, Celia slips up in their little charade, calling Rosalind (who is supposed to be her brother Ganymede) "Cousin Ganymede." Celia's little slip comes out only in her excited panic over Rosalind fainting.
- 4.3.161: Celia helps Ganymede get home, as the "boy" is looking paler and paler. Her last line in the play is, fittingly, directed toward Oliver, to whom she says, "Good sir, go with us."

Oliver Character Analysis

Oliver de Boys is the oldest son of Sir Rowland de Boys, and the elder brother of our hero Orlando. From the beginning, all we really know about Oliver is that he's kind of a jerkosaur. He denies his brother his inheritance, and then he tries to kill him, and then he says he never loved him. Not exactly a Boy Scout. Because he's so villainous, Oliver is rather different than the rest of the play's good-natured characters. Yet it's important to note that Oliver is not entirely an anomaly; like all the other characters, Oliver acts on his deep-seated feelings – even if he can't rationalize them. It's just that most people in the play are driven by their feelings of hate for his brother Orlando.

Oliver (like our other antagonist, Duke Frederick) is Shakespeare's nod to the fact that passion exists in a spectrum, from fury to tomfoolery. If we didn't have characters like Oliver and Duke Frederick to lend their perspective, we could dismiss the other characters' passion as an adorable homage to the foolishness of love. Instead, we're reminded that passion can be dangerous, that violence comes as easily as mirth when a person driven by his feelings. As Shakespeare presents us with two disparate sides of the spectrum, we can take each of them more seriously, as one without the other would just be unbelievable.

However, because the play is a comedy and needs a happy ending, the mean-spirited Oliver ends up transformed by his forest experience (and his brother's kindness) into being a good guy. (Interestingly, in saving Oliver, Orlando acted on his feelings – had he been led by his reason, he would've gladly let Oliver be eaten.) But Oliver isn't transformed into being a rational. Instead, he falls immediately and inexplicably in love with Aliena, and he's so changed that he'd be willing to live the life of a poor shepherd.

In keeping up this romantic and passionate outlook in the character of Oliver, the play remains

consistent. But the presence of the antagonists (and their antagonism) may be a subtle suggestion that passion can't be the only guiding force in our lives – even if it makes for good theater.

Oliver Timeline and Summary

- 1.1.29: Oliver approaches Orlando, who has been chatting with Adam, the family servant. Oliver asks Orlando what he's been making, which means "what are you doing?" or possible "how's it hangin'?"
- 1.1.31: Orlando plays on the meaning of "making," and says he hasn't been taught to make anything. Oliver, undeterred, asks what he's been marring (or destroying, as Orlando hasn't been making anything).
- 1.1.35: Oliver responds that Orlando should spend his time more wisely than his current idling about, and basically tells him to go to hell.
- 1.1.40: As Orlando goes on about his poor condition at Oliver's hand, Oliver asks if he knows where he is and to whom he's talking, essentially saying, "I'm kind of a big deal."
- 1.1.52: As Orlando continues to be saucy by claiming he has as much of his father in him as his brother does, Oliver gets upset. He hits Orlando, and when his brother fights back, calls him a villain for laying hands on him. He demands that Orlando let him go.
- 1.1.75: As Orlando asks for his portion of inheritance so he can leave, Oliver asks just what he plans to do. He says perhaps Orlando will beg after his inheritance is spent. Oliver promises he won't be bothered by his brother for long, ominously saying Orlando will get what's coming to him. Oliver asks Orlando to leave him alone.
- 1.1.81: Oliver bids Adam, the faithful old servant, to go with Orlando, calling him an "old dog."
- 1.1.85: Once Orlando and Adam have left, Oliver notes that Orlando is getting too big for his britches. Oliver declares that he'll cure Orlando of his bad attitude, and won't give him his portion of the inheritance either.
- 1.1.89: Oliver calls in his servant, Dennis. He asks Dennis to call in Charles, the Duke's wrestler, who had come to see Oliver. As Dennis leaves to get Charles, Oliver cryptically says that that the wrestling will be a good way, and we all wonder, "a good way to do *what* ?"
- 1.1.96: Oliver greets Charles warmly and asks for the news at court. Hearing about the scandal of Duke Frederick unseating Duke Senior, Oliver asks if Rosalind will be banished with her father and wonders where her father will go.
- 1.1.120: Oliver asks whether Charles will wrestle tomorrow before Duke Frederick.
- 1.1.137: Charles says he *will* wrestle tomorrow, and that's exactly what he came to see Oliver about. Charles has heard that Orlando intends to challenge him at wrestling, and worrying that Orlando is but a little slip of a thing, Charles really doesn't want to have to crush him to a pulp. Charles came hoping to get Oliver to dissuade Orlando from fighting. Hearing all of this, Oliver says he's grateful for Charles's love to him and will reward it well. Oliver then lies, saying that he has already tried to dissuade his brother from fighting. Oliver also says his brother wouldn't be swayed, as he's the most stubborn boy in all of France. Oliver then says all sorts of nasty (and seemingly untrue) things about Orlando. He

claims that Orlando is ambitious, envious, and constantly plotting against Oliver, even though he is his "natural brother." Oliver advises Charles to use his discretion, saying he would as willingly have Charles break Orlando's neck as his finger. Oliver warns Charles further, saying if Orlando's done any disgrace by Charles, he won't stop until he's done some great harm to Charles in return, including but not limited to poison, entrapment, and leading Charles to suicide. Oliver claims it hurts his heart to say it, but Orlando is the most villainous youth alive, and possible the most villainous ever. Oliver adds that these nasty descriptions are actually softened because he's Orlando's brother. If he told Charles about the *real* Orlando, it would make him weep and Charles pee in his pants. (We know, of course, that none of this is true, and that Oliver is the real villain.)

- 1.1.163: And yet, in case we didn't know, Oliver reveals his true intentions after Charles leaves. He says he hopes to see Orlando's end tomorrow (as he is crushed and killed by Charles, no doubt). Oliver admits that he doesn't know why, but deep in his soul, he hates Orlando more than anything. Oliver then lists all of Orlando's good traits – he has a gentlemanly character and is smart even though he's never been to school. Orlando is noble and well-liked by all, especially those who know him best. For all these reasons, Oliver knows he's wrong to hate his brother. Still, he's got a better solution than having to deal with his feelings, he'll just have Charles kill Orlando instead. Now, all he has to do is encourage his brother to go and fight Charles.

- 3.1.13: Oliver has just been berated by Duke Frederick about Orlando. The Duke demands that Oliver bring Orlando to him, dead or alive. If Oliver doesn't, Duke Frederick promises to raise hell for Oliver. Oliver responds by saying he wishes the Duke knew that Oliver never loved his brother in all his life.

- 4.3.75: Oliver comes upon Celia and Ganymede in the forest, and describes a house he's looking for (which is their house, unbeknownst to him).

- 4.3.83: As Celia speaks to him, Oliver recognizes the pair as those described to him by Orlando; he realizes they are whom he's looking for. Oliver doesn't mince words and reveals that he was told that the boy looks like a girl, and that his sister is brown and short.

- 4.3.91: After Celia's confirmed that it is their house he's seeking, Oliver says he's come to bring Orlando's regards to them both. For the boy Orlando calls Rosalind, he brings a bloody handkerchief.

- 4.3.95: Rosalind asks what they're supposed to think about the whole bloody handkerchief drop-off. Oliver replies they'd find his shame in it, if they knew who he was, and how, why, and where the handkerchief came to be full of blood.

- 4.3.98: Celia asks if Oliver won't tell the darn story already, instead of being such a drama-queen. Oliver sums up that Orlando found a wretched and ragged man sleeping under an old oak tree. A green snake had wrapped itself around the man's neck, and was poised to bite him in the mouth. Fortunately for everyone except the hungry snake, the serpent saw Orlando coming and slithered away under a bush. Then, under the very same bush, a lioness was crouched and waiting for the sleeping man to stir (as lionesses like their prey to seem alive). Orlando saw this, went closer to the man to wake him, and saw that it was in fact his wicked brother Oliver.

- 4.3.124: Celia chimes in that she'd heard of that brother, and Orlando said he was pretty vile. Oliver (knowing she's talking about him, even if she doesn't know it) says Orlando was right to call his brother vile, for even he (the story teller, the yet-to-be revealed Oliver) knows the man was vile.

- 4.3.127: Rosalind, unlike the interrupting Celia, wants Oliver to continue the story, and

asks whether Orlando left his wicked brother to his lioness-food fate. Oliver says that twice Orlando tried to leave, but his kindness got the better of his desire for revenge, and his nature was stronger than this opportunity to see his brother eaten by a wild creature. So, Orlando turned back and fought the lioness, quickly defeating her. The tussle of course awakened the sleeping man. Now the storyteller delivers the punch line: the sleeping man was none other than himself. Which means he's Oliver. Surprise!

- 4.3.135: The girls are shocked, and ask whether it was this man before them, who they now know to be Oliver, who tried so often to kill Orlando. Oliver admits it *was* him, but it isn't him now. He says he's not ashamed to tell them that it was him, as he's since transformed into a new (and better) man, and he feels pretty awesome about it. (It's nice to not want to murder your brother in cold blood anymore.)

- 4.3.138: Rosalind yearns for Oliver to quickly explain the bloody handkerchief. Oliver says that after he and his brother tearfully recounted how Oliver came to the forest, Orlando led him to Duke Senior. The Duke took good care of Oliver, and then gave him over to his loving brother. Orlando took Oliver back to his cave and stripped to reveal that the lioness had taken a healthy piece of Orlando's arm. Turns out, Orlando had been bleeding this whole time and just sucking it up. After revealing his wound, Orlando cried out "Rosalind!" and then fainted from blood loss. As Oliver bound up his wound, Orlando asked him to go to Ganymede and explain the generally stellar excuse he has for being absent.

- 4.3.158: Oliver responds with tact to Ganymede's fainting spell. He tells Celia that many people faint when they look at blood.

- 4.3.163: Yet as Ganymede recovers, Oliver chides him. He declares, a little incredulously, that Ganymede is supposed to be a man, yet he lacks a man's heart.

- 4.3.169: Ganymede tries to assure Oliver that his fainting was all part of the act of pretending to be Rosalind, but Oliver sees right through it. He says the faint wasn't fake at all, as Ganymede's complexion shows real passion.

- 4.3.173: As Ganymede again assures the faint was fake, Oliver says Ganymede should keep faking and pretend to be a man. (He's onto something here...)

- 4.3.179: As Celia invites Oliver back to her place with the fainting Ganymede, Oliver says he'll go with them. He says he needs to bring word back to Orlando that Rosalind excuses him. Oliver calls Ganymede "Rosalind" here, which either means he's playing along, or that he actually knows what's up.

- 5.2.5: Orlando questions Oliver on how he could've fallen in love with Aliena (Celia) so fast. (This is how we find out Oliver and Celia have fallen in love, by the way.) Oliver asks that Orlando not consider how foolish the whole thing seems, and then lists off why it's foolish: the rashness of the decision, Aliena's poverty, the short time they've known each other, how quickly Oliver courted Aliena, and how quickly she accepted. After listing that all off, Oliver asks that his brother ignore these concerns and simply give him and Aliena (Celia) his blessing. He points out that it will be to Orlando's advantage to give his blessing: if Oliver marries Aliena, he'll give up their father's estate and money to Orlando and live in the forest as a poor shepherd with his love. (Ah, *l'amour*.)

- 5.2.18: Oliver's last line in the play is cheeky; Ganymede enters to tend to Orlando, and as Oliver is leaving, Ganymede says a polite "God save you, brother." Oliver responds with "And you, fair sister," possibly playing along with Orlando and Ganymede's pretend game, possibly outing Ganymede as a woman.

Character Roles

Protagonist

Rosalind

Rosalind is the central point around which the play pivots. Early on in the story, it's her plight that connects all the main characters (her father, her cousin, the boy who loves her). As she begins to realize this power, she acts more and more deliberately to get the outcomes she wants. Rosalind is definitely one of Shakespeare's most fully realized female characters, as well as the one with the greatest number of lines. Further, Rosalind has no limitations on her interaction with anyone – she is both a boy and a girl, a country youth and a court noble, a cynical wit and a starry-eyed lover. The flexibility of her character allows us to see more facets of her surrounding cast and deeper into her own character at the same time.

Antagonist

Duke Frederick

Duke Frederick is the wayward Duke who's the main source of trouble for our heroine. We know Duke Frederick is a bad guy as soon as we meet him – he's unseated his own brother for the dukedom, and seems unconcerned that Duke Senior now has to live in the forest like a vagabond. When Duke Frederick brings his wrath down on Rosalind, he acts much the same way Oliver de Boys (our other antagonist) does – his anger comes from a jealousy that has no basis in reason. Rosalind hasn't done him any wrong, but he'll victimize her anyway, accusing her of a potential for treachery though she's shown no signs of it. Still, there's an upside to all this inexplicable anger: if Duke Frederick hates Rosalind for what is really no good reason, then we're not surprised when he has the sudden turn-around required of villains in comedies. Who has time for bad-guys with a back-story?

Antagonist

Oliver

Oliver de Boys has the same problem as Duke Frederick: his brother is too nice. Rather than becoming nicer, he decides the answer is to get rid of his brother. This approach makes Oliver de Boys the main antagonist of our hero Orlando. Oliver even admits that he hates his brother for no reason, but because of his power, no reason is reason enough to murder Orlando. Oliver might be like Duke Frederick in lashing out at a threat to his power, but there's another component to Oliver's hatred: he is simply jealous. Orlando, rather than reasoning with his brother, gets angry, which means Oliver never sees any of the goodness and kindness that Orlando is so well loved for. It makes sense then, that Oliver finally becomes a good person when he's persuaded by Orlando's kind act later in the play (protecting Oliver from a lioness). Again, villains in comedies can't *really* be bad, because that'd be too serious. Oliver's quick turn-around shows us that Oliver was just acting out of misunderstanding (a force that often drives Shakespeare's comedies).

Foil

A Note For You

The play is essentially made up of foils. At all points, conversations occur, and then are followed up by essentially the same conversations by different characters with different perspectives. We

could think of how Ganymede is a foil to Silvius, or Audrey to Celia (in their willingness to give up their love quickly), or come up with any number of foils, but for now we'll talk about the most important two and let you do the rest.

Foil
Duke Senior to Duke Frederick
Duke Senior is obviously more mature than Frederick. (Or else he wouldn't be named "Senior.") Senior is happy in the forest, reminded of how nice it is to live in one big snowy reality check, free from flattery and treachery. Frederick, by contrast, is consumed by the treachery he's committed, and is worried it'll work against him. He sends Rosalind out on the street for no reason other than his worry that she might one day turn out to be a traitor. He's ready to go after Oliver because of his connection to the boy's long-dead father.

Foil
Oliver to Orlando
Oliver shares Duke Frederick's paranoid treachery when it comes to his brother, Orlando. Oliver would've lured Orlando into a death trap, yet Orlando actively works to save his brother even at the risk of his own life. When faced with the good Orlando has done for him, Oliver is so shocked by his own cowardly and paranoid actions that he has a change of heart, much like Duke Frederick eventually does.

Foil
Jaques to Touchstone
These two men are basically two different versions of the same guy. Where Touchstone is full of silliness, Jaques is full of weighty melancholy. Neither man can really be taken seriously because they're on the "abominable extremes" that Rosalind earlier pointed out to be, well, abominable. On the other hand, because we're so accustomed to a particular type of speech out of each character, it's noticeable when they speak differently from their stereotype and suggest they might be more than just an archetype. Though it seems Jaques and Touchstone have different outer shells (one of humor, the other of dolor), they both use these shells to protect themselves from criticism and observation. Most importantly, both men bust out with little glints of wisdom from time to time, lending the play its Jack Handy-style "Deep Thoughts."

Character Clues

Social Status or Societal Position
The pastoral setting should free us from having to worry about the constraints of the court. Still, many of the court's characters carry the own arrogance of their titles into the forest with them. Note how Touchstone greets Corin, a stranger to him, when he is in dire need of some hospitality:

TOUCHSTONE
Holla, you clown!
ROSALIND
Peace, fool; he's not thy kinsman.

CORIN
Who calls?
TOUCHSTONE
Your betters, sir.
CORIN
Else are they very wretched.

Touchstone is in turn put down. When Jaques introduces him to Duke Senior, Jaques laughs heartily at the idea that Touchstone had been "at court." Jaques knows Touchstone's court position as a lowly fool, and as a lord can stand on it mockingly. The fool is not to be pitied, as he did the same thing to poor Corin, who was guilty only of being unschooled in the way of the court. Being so ignorant of court ways, all Corin can tell is that anyone from court is higher than he, and rather than reply as a free man of the forest, he subjects himself to the fool. Status only matters if those around you think it matters, too.

Interestingly, it is those with the most claim to titles that are most humble about it in the forest. Rosalind considers herself an exile more than a princess, and becomes happily involved in love-matches over things like court-matches (which aim for prestige instead of warm and fuzzy feelings). Orlando, while he originally wanted education and training befitting a gentleman, conspires with Adam to seek a lowly life of contentment in the forest. Even when Jaques would have him commiserate about the world, Orlando says he thinks ill of none but himself, whom he knows best. This is pretty significant, as both his experience and his status as a nobleman would easily let him condescend to others. Yet the exiled Duke might be the best example of grace under lost titles. When we meet the Duke, he says he's glad to leave the pomp of the court, as it is in the forest that he is reminded he's only one of many men on earth:

And churlish chiding of the winter's wind,
Which when it bites and blows upon my body,
Even till I shrink with cold, I smile and say
'This is no flattery; these are counsellors
That feelingly persuade me what I am.'

It seems Shakespeare is using status as a mark, both of nobility and of shame. Those who actually deserve their noble titles would let them drop away upon entry to Arden; their graciousness and nobility is in their nature. The others who would cling to their tiles, or judge others by them, are less to be respected, as they've learned less (and are worth less) in both settings.

Literary Devices

Symbols, Imagery, Allegory

Prodigal Son
The Biblical parable of the Prodigal Son works in this play on a variety of levels. The parable

begins with a man who has two sons. The younger asks for his share of his inheritance and leaves for a distant country, where he lives pretty cushy in a sex, drugs, and rock 'n roll lifestyle. It's all good until the foreign land has a famine and the younger son hires himself out to a private citizen and ends up feeding pigs. The boy is so hungry that he wishes for the pigs' food, but he's short on charity from everyone – even the pigs. He comes to his senses under these hard conditions, and decides to go back to his father and apologize, repenting of his bad behavior. Before he can even get his apology out, his father has spotted him on the road and killed the best calf for him, rejoicing that he's returned.

Meanwhile the older brother, who's been good this whole time, hasn't gotten so much as a goat to have a little celebratory (goat-eating) time with his friends. Angry, the older brother resents his father's treatment of the naughty younger brother. Finally, the father explains his behavior to the older brother: what's his father's is his, as he's always been good. But still, they need to celebrate the return of the younger brother. He was dead to them, and on his return has come back to life. He was lost, but on coming back home, he's been found. This is the prodigal son story in the Bible.

So back to the Bard: Orlando makes the most direct reference to the story in the first scene of the first act: "Orlando: Shall I keep your hogs, and eat husks with them? What prodigal portion have I spent that I should come to such penury?" Prodigal is an unusual enough word, but the hog-eating detail is pretty specific. Orlando strikes out at his older brother and draws a contrast between himself and the actual prodigal son, who has done all sorts of wrong whereas Orlando feels he's done none.

The story works on a variety of other levels too. Oliver, like the older brother of the prodigal son, resents the celebration of his brother. Oliver is jealous of how well-received and good his brother is. In the Bible, only when the brother vents his rage does he hear that he, too, will gain much from his father. In our plot, once Oliver has decided that Orlando can have all their father's property (in recognition of Oliver's bad behavior), Jaques de Boys delivers the good news that Orlando will be Duke Senior's successor. So in the end, Oliver can actually take back his father's land in good conscience, and everyone is happy.

You've also got this whole aspect of forgiveness; the prodigal son doesn't have time to apologize to his father before his father embraces him. Orlando, who has been turned out and plotted against by his brother, saves Oliver's life while he sleeps – before his brother has a chance to apologize. As in the Biblical parable, Orlando acted before he even heard his brother speak; he just did the noble thing.

Animals

As You Like It takes place in a forest, and as we all know, forests are great places for exiled dukes, court fools, and adoring lovers to hang out. But let us not forget the original inhabitants, and how everyone sets them out to slaughter, usurps their lands, and then pretends to be really, really sorry while still reaping the benefits. Animals, as Jaques points out, are the original inhabitants of this pleasant "uninhabited" forest the court-people have chanced upon, and they end up being central symbols in much of the text. Jaques anthropomorphizes a fallen deer, all awash in tears. He characterizes the callous deer-brethren that walk on by just like the mean courtiers who'll not note when a fellow is down, except to kick him (or in the case of the deer,

prance over its bleeding carcass). Also, it's pretty shady stuff that the exiles should come to another place and make exiles of the other folks that live there. Orlando also gets some animal imagery - his brother Oliver is threatened by a snake at the mouth while sleeping.

As any good student of English knows, any time there's a snake, the author has to say something about the Bible. There's the issue of the serpent betraying Eve's trust (as Oliver did to Orlando, luring him home to broil him) but there's also the issue of Oliver suffering because he did a deliberately bad thing by sending his brother out (just as Eve offered the apple to Adam despite warnings from God). The snake at the mouth can also stand for the horrible things Oliver has said. Like what? Well, like when he told Duke Frederick that he never loved his brother. Note that Oliver himself is in the forest while exiled from his earthly paradise (a title, some land, and a secure future). His good brother saves him before the snake bites, which would have meant real exile (from the whole being alive gig). Oliver then realizes the forest is not his exile, but rather his salvation, both morally and insofar as he meets and falls in love with Celia.

Orlando also gets likened to animals. When he goes to collect the starving, aged Adam, he goes "like a doe to her fawn," which is gentle, albeit maternal, imagery. When Rosalind abuses him, she says it would be better if he were a snail come to woo her. Finally, Rosalind falls for Orlando most completely when she hears he's bested a lioness. Though Orlando eventually won the battle, the lioness did get a couple of good swipes at him such that he really does look like he wears his heart on his sleeve. (We're trying to be clever. Orlando's arm is all bloody.) Now, a lioness is very particularly a *female* lion, a ferocious member of the *female* sex, who may be eventually overthrown, but not before she lands some good hits… sound like any major *female* characters in the play to you? Especially ones that Orlando might fight and eventually defeat? (Rosalind.)

Finally, animals are ferocious fornicators, and we as people like to watch and think about that, as witnessed by the proliferation of "nature channels." The play is more than a little littered with animal references as means of comparison to humans playing a bit of skin tag. (Animal imagery is so entrenched that in *Othello*, Shakespeare refers to sex as "making the beast with two backs.") Audrey herds goats, and Touchstone suggests he caper with her, which in Latin means "he-goat." In Shakespeare's day, "he-goat" might allude to "goatish," which meant pure and total lechery. When Touchstone makes up a fake love poem for Rosalind, he refers to her as a cat in heat, a doe to be done by a buck (another allusion to cuckold's horns can be found here), and, moving on to a much more comfortable subject for everyone…a rose.

Rose
Which brings us to the name of our primary character. It's pretty easy to shave "Rosalind" down to "Ros," which if you buy a vowel brings you to "rose," which makes us think of another Shakespeare play, *Romeo and Juliet*. Recall Juliet's famous balcony speech, "What's in a name? That which we call a rose, by any other word would smell as sweet." A rose, at once sweet and thorny, seems to have had particular significance to Shakespeare.

The rose imagery pops up twice in *As You Like It*. Celia, doting, calls her cousin "Rose, my sweet Rose." Touchstone, who does not dote, adds the rose image into his mock love poem of Rosalind. Touchstone quips, "He that sweetest rose will find / Must find love's prick and

Rosalind." So yes, roses are thorny, but this is especially interesting because "prick" is a useful Elizabethan (and current British) slang term for the male penis.

Love has a pricking sting as a rose has a thorn, but Rosalind also has a prick, because she's supposed to be a man. To find Rosalind, you'd also find Ganymede, a man. Still, though, Rosalind isn't really a man. Perhaps it's a metaphor too, and not just an easy way to work in the word "prick." Rosalind *seems* to have a thorny nature, but maybe she'll actually be giddy when in love, and not a mean and ruthless harpy. Rosalind abounds with contradictions – kind of like a rose. Also she's hot, and roses are beautiful things.

Finally, for much of the play, Rosalind cavorts around as the boy named Ganymede. Ganymede was cup-bearer to the god Jove, but also Jove's lover. This false name makes sense, regarding what might be considered a homoerotic relationship between Ganymede and Orlando under false pretences. By her real name, Rosalind, she is just as enticing to Orlando.

Setting

The Forest of Arden, outside the courts of France
Most of the characters in the play are not from the forest, but end up there by dint of one mishap or another. The setting is important as an unfamiliar place for these members of the court. Most importantly, it relaxes the rules of conventional relationships. In the forest, desire rules. Characters have the freedom to be and say and do as they please, whether it's to love easily or lust shamelessly. The forest has magical qualities, like Hymen showing up suddenly at the end (what was up with that?). But mostly, it's the fact of being in a totally new environment that works magic on these characters. If they were in the court, they'd definitely be constrained by court traditions and expectations.

The forest is also a handy foil to the court; not only does it provide freedom, but things here are done almost in direct contrast to the pomp and circumstance of the stuff back home. The natural space of the forest serves to highlight how ridiculous and contrary to human nature the court and its conceits are. It also brings us (and the lovers) back to those birds-and-bees instincts.

Narrator Point of View
Though all works of literature present the author's point of view, they don't all have a narrator or a narrative voice that ties together and presents the story. This particular piece of literature does not have a narrator through whose eyes or voice we learn the story.

Genre

Comedy, Romance, Pastoral
As You Like It is most definitely a comedy, first because it ends in marriage and not murder, and

second because it's pretty funny, as comedies tend to be. Any inclination you had to call it a love story is undercut by the fact that Rosalind, the center of the play, is quick to make fun of love. There's definitely love, but the characters are too self-aware of their own absurdity to be the simpler love-struck stuff of romance.

This comedy also employs elements of the pastoral genre. The setting is unfamiliar to the characters and provides important plot and development points. Characters transform into their real selves when liberated from societal constraints. Further, while the forest allows people to test the limitations of the courtly world, it also lets them get familiar with themselves in unfamiliar ways. In the forest, relationships and philosophy can be examined in natural light, without affectation. Finally, when everybody goes back to court, you know they won't fall into the same patterns because of the valuable lessons they've learned in this more objective sphere.

Tone

Silly, Idea-lite

This play is silly and idea-lite in regards to all the jesting going on. The sheer mass of the play is given over to jokes and silly situations, and you get a sense that not even the dark stuff is that serious, given how quickly the bad characters experience turn-arounds. (Imagine Voldemort being all, "You know, I've had enough of this evil thing. Let's give it up.") Yet the play is more than fluff; philosophical ideas and debate punctuate the other lovelorn nonsense. Big ideas like time, love, mortality, and authority are all discussed in one way or another. They don't seem onerous or overly melodramatic because they've got a healthy dose of comedy mixed in. The ideas are rarely flushed out to boring ends and tiny details, but the characters are smart and charming enough to make sure you don't even really notice that you could get bored learning so much.

Writing Style

Shakespearean-ish

As a work of art, many critics say this isn't Shakespeare's most earth-shattering – but comedy is harder to make truly epic than the tortured dead-dad, suicidal-son, and nation-at-war story. What makes this one a real gem is the incisive and unforgiving wit of most of its characters. The wordplay, especially of Rosalind and Touchstone, and even Celia on occasion, serves to mesmerize the watcher/listener/reader as well as the other characters. Shakespeare may not be dealing directly with heavy issues, but he sure reminds you in every scene that he is THE master of English letters and can make the language do what he pleases. He tells dirty jokes, moralizes on the nature of aging, and gets in a few gaffs on the court and copulating cattle. As an acutely brilliant collection of snappy observations and awkward tensions, this is the Jerry Seinfeld of the Elizabethan age.

What's Up With the Title?

The title is not very direct, which, if you think about it (pause for thinking), is an apt description of the play, too. It could be about exile, love, philosophy, or homosexuality. You take away from it what you want. As a result, the play gets mixed reviews – some people love its clever wordplay and philosophy, while others see it as filler compared to Shakespeare's more serious plays. Author George Bernard Shaw quipped that the play was just a cheap crowd-pleaser, and that the Bard titled the play to mean "As *you* like it" because Shakespeare knew it was not his best work. On the other hand, Harold Bloom, the renowned professor and "anti-literary criticism literary critic," ranks *As You Like It* (along with *Twelfth Night*) as his favorite Shakespeare play for "sheer pleasure." Though he does call the work "zany," his analysis of its poetry and of the wonderful character Rosalind insists that there is much for you to like here – if you are willing to not dismiss it as fluff.

Did You Know?

Trivia

- The beginning of the "All the world's a stage" speech is thought to have been inspired by the motto of the Globe Theater: "*Totus mundus agit histrionem,*" or, "The whole world plays the actor." (Evans, G. Blakemore, The Riverside Shakespeare, 2nd ed., 415)
- *"What's in a name? that which we call a rose / By any other word would smell as sweet…"* A story that circulates around the London tour guide circuit, which may or may not be credible, is that this line in *Romeo and Juliet* is actually making fun of the rival Rose Theater. Due to a lack of effective sanitary technology, the Rose Theater was known for smelling less than rosy. It does add another level to our thinking on Rosalind, this Rose that at once has a penchant for fainting and giddiness, and cruel and saucy words. Roses… complicated stuff.
- According to the history of radio station WCAL in the U.S. state of Minnesota, *As You Like It* may have been the first play ever broadcast. It went over the air in 1922.
- It is traditionally held that Shakespeare himself may have played Adam in early runs of the play. Maybe that explains why Adam curiously disappears during the course of the play – Shakespeare's a busy guy.

Steaminess Rating

PG

As You Like It ends up high on the list of Shakespeare's comedies because of its ideas and its language. While ideas and language don't provide much in the way of the actual sex, they are certainly at the base of how such things happen. Imagination is at the root of sex in the play –

Rosalind has scarcely met Orlando before she's talking about having his babies, though throughout the course of the play they don't once have the occasion to kiss before they get hitched.

Touchstone's own punning provides a fair share of sexual allusion, especially the bit about the codpiece, but the play is focused wholly more on love than on its byproducts. If you want to think about sex, you can imagine all the fun that follows the end of the play.

Allusions and Cultural References

Literature, Philosophy, and Mythology
The Bible: Luke 15 – The Prodigal Son (1.1.47)
Helen of Troy (3.2.145)
Atalanta and her race with Hippomenes (3.2.147)
Lucretia (3.2.148)
Troilus, of Troilus and Cressida (4.1.97)
Hero and Leander (4.1.100): As a side note, the story of Hero and Leander was being expanded into a narrative by Christopher Marlowe, a contemporary of Shakespeare, but the writer died before it was completed.
Cupid (4.1.211)

Historical Figures
Christopher Marlowe: Marlowe was a contemporary of Shakespeare, and hit the big time of London theatre while Shakespeare was still making a name for himself. That's pretty much all we can say with certainty about the man, besides the fact that Marlowe's work, including *Doctor Faustus* and *Tamburlaine*, set him up as one of Elizabethan England's best and brightest. Naturally, there is speculation of a rivalry between the two playwrights (born in the same year, 1564). As Shakespeare was still proving his salt (only a year before, he was lambasted by London playwright Robert Greene as an amateur and "upstart crow"), it only makes sense that Shakespeare would pay homage to Marlowe in this play, written after Marlowe's unsavory death in 1593. As evidenced in *Julius Caesar*, it's a lot easier to praise your competitors after they're dead, so Shakespeare's shout outs to Marlowe are less than subtle and more than significant.

Marlowe was working on a narrative poem of Hero and Leander, but only got to the point where the two are lovers before he died – Rosalind picks up the tale of what happens after that, when Hero is no longer a "nun" of Aphrodite's. Marlowe's poem was finished by George Chapman and published in 1598, about two years before *As You Like It* is thought to have debuted. Marlowe died in 1593. (4.1.100)

Shakespeare has Phebe quote Marlowe. "Dead shepherd, now I find thy saw of might, 'Who ever lov'd that lov'd not at first sight!'" comes from Marlowe's *Hero and Leander*, and the dead shepherd of whom Phebe speaks is, of course, Marlowe himself. (3.5.81)

Touchstone speaks to Phebe: "When a man's verses cannot be understood, nor a man's good wit seconded with the forward child understanding, it strikes a man more dead than a great reckoning in a little room." Some critics find here a reference to Marlowe's death in 1593. It was held that Marlowe had died ("great reckoning") instantly after being stabbed above the eye during a quarrel over the bill in a pub ("little room") (3.3.12). (Evans, G. Blakemore, The Riverside Shakespeare, 2nd ed., 421.)

Best of the Web

Movie or TV Productions
1936 Movie
http://imdb.com/title/tt0027311/
As You Like It, a British production starring Laurence Olivier in his first Shakespearean role for the big screen.

1963 TV Movie
http://imdb.com/title/tt0056837/
A TV version of the play made in the UK, starring Vanessa Redgrave.

1992 Movie
http://imdb.com/title/tt0103723/
Another British production, this one was directed by Christine Edzard and placed the action in modern London, with the Court of France as a flashy office block and the "forest" as the dirty bank of the Thames. Lords are homeless bums, and reviews are mixed.

2006 Movie
http://imdb.com/title/tt0450972/
The most recent film production of the play was Kenneth Branagh's 2006 production, also titled *As You Like It*. This one, though, is set in 19th century Japan during the opening of the nation to the West.

Videos
1936 Film Clip
http://www.youtube.com/watch?v=Yc1r-bd7Jww
Laurence Olivier as Orlando in the 1936 production of the film.

Scene from the 1978 Movie
http://www.youtube.com/watch?v=yhC8YlQ_flQ
Helen Mirren (from *The Queen* and also a killer actress in general) as Rosalind in a 1978 TV production.

Movie Trailer
http://www.youtube.com/watch?v=4JLw0kXO2N4&mode=related&search
The movie trailer for the 2006 film, set in Japan.

Audios

"All the world's stage…"

http://www.britannica.com/eb/art-75832/Jaques-philosophizes-All-the-worlds-a-stage-performed-by-John

John Gielgud reading Jaques's speech, "All the world's a stage…" (2.7.38). Recording made around 1930.

Documents

"Variations on a Theme of Love"

http://www.mala.bc.ca/~johnstoi/eng366/lectures/Ayl.htm

A general introduction to thinking about the context of *As You Like It*, and how it fits within Shakespeare's complete works. This paper definitely hits a lot of the major points of characters and critical issues (language, gender, etc.), but is unique in the discussion of the different types of comedic styles that were cropping up around the time Shakespeare was working on this play.

Complete Online Text of the Play

http://www.opensourceshakespeare.org/views/plays/playmenu.php?WorkID=asyoulikeit

Open Source Shakespeare's full online text of the play, with optional views to see either individual bits or the entire thing as a scrollable document in one fell swoop. The most interesting feature is definitely the listing option to see all the lines of individual characters, which is a cool (but jarring) exercise.

Another Complete Online Text of *As You Like It*

http://www.worldebooklibrary.com/eBooks/Renascence_Editions/shake/ayli.html

Project Gutenberg's full online text of the play, without breaks or line numbers.

Websites

The Royal Shakespeare Company: *As You Like It*

http://www.rsc.org.uk/asyoulikeitpack/about/whoswho.html

The Royal Shakespeare Company's (RSC) compact and interesting site on *As You Like It*, centered around their 2003 production of the play. It is especially illuminating as to theater productions of the play throughout history, and it's full of tidbits of campy gossip for those who care for that sort of thing. Also, lots of great historic photos of the play in production at RSC and the connections between the players. (See "Who's who.")

PBS Shakespeare

http://www.pbs.org/shakespeare/works/work182.html

PBS' site devoted to its own investigation of Shakespeare. There's great background stuff on Shakespeare in general and a very helpful aggregation of Shakespearean words and historically relevant information, if that's your cup of tea.

Printed in Great Britain
by Amazon